Building Robust Competencies

Paul C. Green

Building Robust Competencies

Linking Human Resource Systems to Organizational Strategies

Jossey-Bass Publishers
San Francisco

Jossey-Bass books and products are available through most bookstores. To contact
Jossey-Bass directly, call (888) 378-2537, fax to (800) 605-2665, or visit our website
at www.josseybass.com.

Substantial discounts on bulk quantities of Jossey-Bass books are available to
corporations, professional associations, and other organizations. For details and
discount information, contact the special sales department at Jossey-Bass.

Epigraph for Chapter One from E. E. Lawler and G. Ledford, "New Approaches
to Organizing Competencies: Capabilities and the Decline of the Bureaucratic Model."
In C. Cooper and S. Jackson (Eds.). *Creating Tomorrow's Organizations: A Handbook
for Future Research in Organizational Behavior.* Copyright © 1997 by John Wiley & Sons
Limited. Reproduced with permission.

Epigraph quote in Chapter Eight reprinted with permission from Mager, R. F. *Preparing
Instructional Objectives.* Copyright © 1997 by The Center for Effective Performance,
2300 Peachford Road, Suite 2000, Atlanta, GA 30338, 1-800-558-4237.

 Manufactured in the United States of America on Lyons Falls Turin Book.
This paper is acid-free and 100 percent totally chlorine-free.

Library of Congress Cataloging-in-Publication Data

Green, Paul, date.
    Building robust competencies / Paul C. Green.—1st ed.
    p. cm.
    Includes bibliographical references and index.
    ISBN 0-7879-4649-4 (acid-free paper)
    1. Personnel management.   2. Organizational effectiveness.
3. Performance.   I. Title.
    HF5549.G687 1999
    658.3—dc21
                                               98-40230

FIRST EDITION
HB Printing   10 9 8 7 6 5 4 3 2

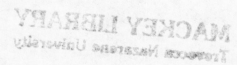

Contents

Figures and Exhibits

Figures

Exhibits

To our mom, whose robust competencies
in commitment, style, integrity, humor, and support
gave our family a loving advantage

Preface

This book explains how to use behavioral competencies to link human resource (HR) systems to an organization's purpose. This linkage will help organizations better communicate to associates about how they can effectively guide their own actions.

The book is written for human resource professionals, who strive to link their organization's core competencies, capabilities, values, and priorities to its human resource applications. For example, you will see how to reflect an organization's core values in job-related interviews, appraisal, coaching, and training.

You can expect this book to recognize and reinforce important distinctions between an organization's strategic core competencies and its individual competencies and skills. Although these distinctions are obvious to business strategists, they are a source of confusion for many in human resources who want to use competencies to reflect vision, culture, and values.

To some extent, this book developed from one of my own mistakes as a consultant. About twenty years ago, I wrote a competency containing this phrase: "Adopt a problem-solving attitude in resolving interpersonal conflict." I knew exactly what that statement meant to me. However, it caused confusion when it was used by a small group in a training class. I was asked, "What does someone do when using a problem-solving attitude?"

So we took the time to develop behavioral descriptions of what we would see or hear when "a problem-solving attitude" was being used. This turned out to be a good learning experience, particularly for me. I realized that I would have done a better job in designing the materials in the first place if I had more clearly defined exactly what to rate. An idea becomes *robust* when we are able to see or hear the actions that define it.

This experience and others like it have helped shape the message of this book: Use behavioral language to build robust core competencies, capabilities, core values, priorities, and skills that describe, guide, and link actions at work.

- By describing what *was done,* we are better able to measure and predict in interviews and performance management.

- By describing what *is being done,* we are better able to coach and train.

- By describing what *needs to be done,* we define selection standards, performance expectations, coaching goals, and instructional objectives.

Behavioral language helps us be specific about what we mean to say.

From another perspective, this is a book about *alignment,* that is, helping individuals see how their actions relate to their organization's identity. This concern stems from the practical question asked by managers: "How do I get everyone marching in the same direction at the same time?"

One of most proven ways to get alignment is to get people to participate in decision making. This *participation* leads to an exchange of information, an opportunity for commitment, and higher performance. Participation builds personal alignment between an individual and the organization.

In this book I refer continuously to the strategic value of participation in generating alignment. However, I describe a different way to build and reinforce alignment. This approach begins by using behavioral language to describe an organization's identity. Traditional components of identity—vision, mission, and values/culture— are converted to behavioral language that describes what needs to be done to link an organization's identity to interviews, appraisal, coaching, and training. This process requires that individuals participate in shaping mission statements, writing structured interviews, developing appraisal forms, setting coaching goals, and creating instructional objectives.

The idea behind this technique is painfully simple. The words that describe the purpose of the organization and the requirements of jobs are included in the forms and procedures that are used to select, appraise, coach, and train. Getting people to talk the same language begins with making it easy for everyone to use the same words and meanings that honestly characterize their organization and its jobs.

Individual competencies are also used to link human resource applications to each other. This approach borrows from the content validation techniques used in developing psychological tests. The same or similar wording is repeatedly used in individual competencies for interviewing, coaching, and training. In other words, the terms in an individual competency that are used for interviewing candidates for a job are also used in the procedures for appraising, coaching, and training the person who is hired for the job.

From another perspective, this is a book about making productive change happen in an organization. How does one use a human resources system to get a critical mass of people on the job to talk about new ways of doing things? The approach offered here is to use the same language repeatedly to make important standards, expectations, guidelines, and objectives a regular part of everyday conversations at work.

To best communicate these ideas, I have chosen to write about the linkage of HR systems at the expense of describing the skills used to make the systems work. For example, I didn't mention probing skills when interviewing, relationship skills in appraisal, listening skills for coaching, or presentation skills with training. I elected also to limit the types of HR applications covered. I feel that the footprint of this approach to linkage can be applied to compensation, labor relations, and other HR initiatives. However, these topics are best explored by those who know more about them than I do.

Although much of the information in this book is derived from research, the book is not a report of research findings. It contains examples of competency *applications* found in presentations, published papers, public information, and articles. Others came from my own experiences as a consultant.

This is a book for the practitioner, and it is written in an accessible style, with key ideas highlighted with "pull outs" from the text. Although some references are available for the reader who wants more detail, the book primarily reflects my opinions on the best way to build and use robust competencies.

The book consistently reflects a behavioral approach instead of the more current, cognitive approach in psychology. Some managers, consultants, and professors may disagree with my emphasizing behavior-based performance skills over traits and attributes. However, my decision to write a practical book led me consciously to argue for simple ideas that will work for a practitioner rather than present information that is theoretically elegant.

I hope that I have expressed these ideas with enough passion to reflect my confidence in this approach without appearing to be personally critical of those who disagree with me.

February 1999   Paul C. Green
Memphis, Tennessee

Acknowledgments

Many people have contributed to this book. On the personal side, my wife has been a source of support and a conceptual stimulator. Instead of commenting on my tendency to be preoccupied with my work, she drew me into the "now" with stimulating conversation and innumerable suggestions on how I could make the book better.

From the business perspective, the customers of Behavioral Technology fueled me with the difficult questions that led me to believe that the time was right for this book. My colleagues at work tolerated my incessant questions, supplied me with ample criticism, and demanded that I be practical.

There is also a more academic domain for gratitude. Victor Balderige continued in the role he filled as my college roommate. Both then and now, he served as a confident guide to clarity when I was on the edge of confusion. Specifically, he helped me identify my audience and be direct with my ideas. Richard Boyatzis offered encouragement beyond my expectations and fueled my energy to go beyond the early draft stage. Michael Campion was a well-informed source of personal encouragement and empirical wisdom. He reassured me about my writing style and guided me to new resources on competencies. Gerry Ledford introduced me to some of his unpublished work on competency development and gave me the courage I needed to say exactly what I thought without apology. And the practical guidance of George Morrisey helped keep me from straying too far in developing ideas around vision, mission, and values.

To the many contributors I have not mentioned here, I will thank you personally the next time we meet.

Thank you all.

The Author

Paul Green is an industrial organizational psychologist with over thirty years of experience in training and consulting. He has worked with a variety of organizations, ranging from small entrepreneurial companies to very large international organizations. He is founder and CEO of Behavioral Technology®, a division of Provant, a training solutions firm with over one thousand associates servicing a broad array of businesses and government agencies.

Paul's primary area of professional practice has been in the assessment of job candidates through the use of tests and interviews. Over a twenty-year period, he has conducted approximately five thousand selection interviews on candidates for a broad range of positions. In addition, he is an active trainer and consultant.

Based on his experience in assessment, he developed the Behavioral Interviewing® Seminar, which has been attended by several hundred thousand managers worldwide. His interviewing techniques were adapted into *More Than a Gut Feeling,* which was recognized by *Fortune* magazine as being one of the all-time best-selling training videos in any category. His book *Get Hired! Winning Strategies to Ace the Interview* (1996) is the authoritative resource for candidates preparing for behavior-based interviews.

In 1998, Behavioral Technology was merged with six other training firms into Provant, which is currently traded as "PROVANT" on the NASDAQ Exchange. This was the first roll-up of performance-skills training companies in this $60 billion industry. Paul serves on the board of directors of Provant while continuing to perform as CEO of Behavioral Technology.

Your comments and questions are welcome. Feel free to correspond: Paul C. Green, Behavioral Technology, 6260 Poplar, Memphis, TN 38119 (e-mail: paulg@btweb.com). Additional information on Behavioral Technology is available at www.btweb.com.

Building Robust
Competencies

Part I
Clarifying Competencies

Who are we, and where are we going? How can we get there faster, better, and cheaper? What are our core competencies? Today, these questions of identity, process, and strategy are not just important for success, they are critical for survival. These challenges are intensified by globalization, technology, and the evolution of a democratic world. The speed of change in these areas is making conceptual leadership more important while reducing the time available for critical thinking.

The times call for robust solutions to practical problems. A *robust solution* is one that stands the test of practical application in a changing world. A robust idea works even though individuals and organizations aren't perfect. Just as a robust athlete can deliver results away from the home, in bad conditions, and with a bothersome injury, a robust solution can deliver results when people are overworked, politics are churning, and resources are limited.

Behavioral competencies are robust. They have been around for over thirty years and have met the ultimate test—they are useful. The use of robust competencies in your organization can be hobbled, however, by abstract language and by personality traits. To build robust human resource competencies you must be able to state them in a way that is reliably understood by most people in your place of work.

Part One sets the stage for building robust competencies by identifying the ambiguities, challenges, and rewards of using competencies (Chapter One). Chapter Two clarifies what is meant by a *competency* and its surrounding concepts. Important distinctions are made between core competencies, capabilities, core values, priorities, technical skills, and performance skills. Chapter Three argues that robust competencies can be defined in terms of the operations that need to be taken to enable you to see or hear them being used. Finally, Chapter Four introduces the use of behavior-based competencies to link an organization's identity to HR systems.

1

Robust Competencies

Adapting to Change Through
Linked Human Resource Systems

*A competency-based human resource management
system . . . represents nothing short of a reinvention
of the practice of human resource management.*
                    Edward Lawler and Gerald Ledford,
                    in Creating Tomorrow's Organizations

Many people today go to work without knowing what will meet
them at the door. Technological advances, globalization, and
innovation are making worklife change so fast that to be organized,
reasonable, and calm is next to impossible.

Let me speculate for a few moments about what you probably
experience on the job. You have more problems than ever. On a
good day, you can turn your problems into challenges. The reality
of where you are right now, however, is deep in the middle of
change—accelerating change. Your skills are becoming more obso-
lete, the demands on you are multiplying, and you can't even find
time to take your cat to the vet. Along with the pressure of doing
your job, there are rumors about what will change next at your office
and who will change with it.

The phone rings. It's your boss. He begins the conversation with
a compliment, which immediately makes you suspicious. Then you
hear him say that you have been volunteered for a task force being

formed to redesign the organization and improve performance since the last restructuring. Oh boy . . . more work!

Later, you interview a candidate who has the unique qualifications you need for a position that has been empty for months. But one of your colleagues gives a "thumbs down." He admits that he can't put his finger on why he came to this conclusion, but he nevertheless boasts about his "gut feeling" in assessing people. The meeting runs into overtime, so the notion of going to lunch is replaced with a can of microwave chili that you throw down while standing in the hall.

Something similar happens in a discussion of your performance. Your boss can't justify an average rating with specific information; instead he says that this is only his "opinion." Even though you get a healthy raise, it's a demotivator. In your heart you know that your boss hasn't really even noticed what you are doing. Oh well, you sigh, he's busy, too.

The same thing happens again and again. It's not just in selection and appraisal. People get coaching without specifics, training without objectives, and rewards without results. And the ambiguity associated with change doesn't help one bit. A lack of clarity makes many decisions that should be routine very slippery. New and unspoken rules on how you should do your job make you feel that you are going out on a limb every time that you offer an opinion. You try to be optimistic—that's your typical approach to problems. But from time to time you wish there were a way to reduce the pressure that you feel while helping your organization be more effective. This is where robust competencies come to help you.

The Competency Solution

Robust competencies can help you solve many of the work problems you experience. There is a competency solution to ambiguity. It isn't perfect. But it does offer a reasonable way to reduce many of the personal stresses you feel at work. A human resources system can use competencies to make it clear what actions need to be taken to do a job well.

What Is a Competency?

The word *competency* is used in very different ways by HR experts and business strategists. We'll explore these uses in the next few paragraphs to establish a common ground for discussing how competencies reduce ambiguity at work. In Chapter Two I offer a more complete definition, presenting the meanings and the special terms that I use in the remainder of the book.

HR practitioners often think of a competency as describing the characteristics of a person. Here is a definition of this use: *An individual competency is a written description of measurable work habits and personal skills used to achieve a work objective.* For example, ideas around leadership, creativity, or presentation skills might be expanded into competency definitions.

Several components of this usage warrant additional comment.

- An *individual competency* is different from *organizational* competencies, capabilities, values, and priorities.

- A *written description* of at least twenty words communicates exactly what is meant by the competency.

- *Measurable work habits and personal skills* means that the competency can be used to measure reliably and predict accurately a person's actions.

- *Individual competencies* contribute to achieving a work objective, but they are often part of a work system that may be the primary cause of the results gained.

Here is an example of an individual competency needed for communicating with team members.

Team communications: Able to ask questions about the quality of work in progress; describes and clarifies team roles to be carried out to reach work objectives; restates important ideas to ensure understanding; expresses opinions on work issues to contribute to team performance.

Notice that discussions around this competency statement can reduce some of the ambiguity that a team member may experience.

Human resource professionals typically think of competencies at an individual level whereas business strategists tend to think of them at an organizational level. For example, core competencies and capabilities describe the characteristics of an organization that make it effective. Specifically, *core competencies* are unique bundles of technical knowledge and skills with tools that have an impact on multiple products and services in an organization and provide a competitive advantage in the marketplace. *Capabilities* describe other important things that the organization can do to reach its goals. These ideas, along with core values and priorities, are discussed further in Chapter Two.

Individual and organizational competencies get everyone pointed in the same direction, thus helping you be more effective in avoiding and solving people problems. For example, a structured interview with questions organized around the individual competencies needed for doing a job well gives logic and predictability to the selection process. When the interview is completed, ratings can be made by comparing interview information to qualities needed in the candidate. This structure in gathering information and decision making reduces ambiguity.

Expectations for a performance discussion can be defined through individual competencies. Some of the current disappointment with performance appraisal can be attributed to an inadequate definition of performance expectations. Individual competencies address this issue by providing a way to compare what was done with what was expected.

Coaching goals are important because they identify the areas needing improvement, and are particularly useful when helping an individual deal with sensitive topics. Individual competencies that state clearly what a person needs to do to do a job well help clarify what a coach needs to say. The coach's authority stems from the job requirements rather from personal wisdom.

Individual competencies also link to training. Once it is decided what needs to be learned to do a job, individual competencies suggest the instructional objectives for developing training classes. This linkage gives additional clarity to what needs to be learned and why particular individuals should be in class.

Individual competencies provide structure and standards for human resource systems, thus reducing ambiguity and helping you have good feelings about what you do on the job. They also help you and others align with your organization by contributing to a shared understanding that enables associates to move in the same direction.

Behavioral Language

The best way to word competencies is with behavioral language that describes the things you can see or hear being done. This enables you to describe the actions needed to achieve the organization's purpose or to do a job well. Behavioral language also allows you to verify your understanding of what has been done, is being done, or needs to be done. It is the foundation for getting agreement in the midst of misunderstanding or resistance.

> The word *excellence* has different meanings for different people. You can get agreement on what excellence really means in your organization by asking your associates to describe what a person says or does when performing in an excellent way.

Individual competencies also can be of help when you are dealing with personal conflicts and disagreements. When competencies are behavioral, they contain descriptive words that can help you avoid saying something that you will regret later. And behavioral language can be used in everyday conversations, forms, and procedures at work. I'm talking about using words that cut through the "gobbledygook" that stands in your way of performing at a higher level.

Just then I used a word, *gobbledygook*, that may not be familiar to you. Even so, it probably didn't throw you off track because the words around it give it meaning. Sometimes this approach gets us by just fine, but it's much better to avoid using words that don't have clear meanings. Behavioral language is the best language for building robust competencies because it makes it easier to communicate standards, expectations, goals, and objectives.

> **Robust competencies help you define what was done, what is being done, and what needs to be done.**

Competency Models

Groups of individual competencies are organized into competency models. Some competency models are generic lists of individual characteristics that can be used in HR systems. Other competency models are specially designed for a particular organization or have a strong research basis that goes beyond any one organization (Boyatzis, 1982; Boyatzis, Cowen, and Kolb, 1995; Spencer and Spencer, 1993).

A competency model can be mostly verbal, mostly graphic, or a mixture. Exhibit 1.1 presents a verbal competency model that was adapted from the Secretary's Commission on Achieving Necessary Skills (SCANS) project, which was initiated by the U.S. Department of Labor (U.S. Department of Labor, 1991a; Green, 1996). Leaders from education, business, and industry identified the types of skills that should be taught in public education to prepare individuals

Exhibit 1.1. A Competency Model.

Performance Skills

ADAPTABILITY

Shows resilience: Rebounds from conflict and difficult situations; treats a negative experience as a learning opportunity; responds to time pressures and interpersonal conflicts with problem-solving actions; withholds negative comments and emotional outbursts; is respectful of others, even under pressure.

Accommodates changes: Responds open-mindedly to change initiatives, looking for ways to help the organization; offers opinions about changes in a supportive manner; follows team agreement on changes in ways that help their effectiveness; resists changes that may be unsafe or illegal.

INTERPERSONAL

Participates in teamwork: Works cooperatively with others and contributes to the group with ideas, suggestions, and effort; communicates acceptance or rejection of team commitments; does not talk about team members in a negative manner in their absence; is willing to confront performance problems of the team.

Displays leadership: Communicates thoughts, feelings, and ideas to justify a position; encourages, persuades, or otherwise motivates individuals or groups; challenges existing procedures, policies, or authority responsibly.

Manages conflict: Expresses opinions directly and clearly without abuse or manipulation; listens to the opinions and feelings of others and demonstrates understanding by restating them; communicates disagreement to persons in authority as necessary; accepts negative feedback as a way to learn; negotiates agreements to resolve differences.

Accepts differences: Works effectively with individuals from diverse backgrounds; behaves professionally and supportively when working with men and women from a variety of ethnic, social, and educational backgrounds; avoids using stereotypes when dealing with others; may correct others on the use of slurs and negative comments about other groups.

Provides service: Works and communicates with clients and customers to satisfy their expectations; adapts one's own needs and objectives to help others reach their objectives; presents difficult information in an attention-getting and persuasive manner.

WORK HABITS

Exhibits integrity: Gathers and uses information in ways that respect confidentiality, business ethics, and organizational secrets; makes truthful comments based on verifiable information; avoids using rumor, gossip, and subjective opinions in decision making; is sensitive to perceived integrity issues; produces complete and accurate written documents.

Manages self: Uses standard operating procedures and work instructions to guide own actions without supervision; selects relevant, goal-related activities and ranks them in order of importance; allocates time to activities, and understands, prepares, and follows schedules; periodically makes decisions that are consistent with the job mission but not guided by policy and procedures.

Motivates self and others: Starts own work and gets others started working; commits to a plan of action and shows a willingness to work hard and long to achieve measurable results; completes tasks quickly; competes productively against self, time allocations, and others.

Follows procedures: Understands, follows, and encourages others to follow prescribed policies and procedures, even when it is inconvenient to do so; improves performance by telling others where policies and procedures interfere with productivity.

Technical Knowledge and Job Skills

RESOURCES

Allocates money: Uses or prepares budgets, makes cost and revenue forecasts, keeps detailed records to track budget performance, and makes appropriate adjustments.

Allocates material and facility resources: Acquires, stores, and distributes materials, supplies, parts, equipment, space, or final products to make the best use of them.

Allocates human resources: Assesses knowledge and skills and distributes work accordingly, evaluates performance, and provides feedback.

INFORMATION

Acquires and evaluates information: Identifies need for data, obtains it from existing sources or creates it, and evaluates its relevance and accuracy.

Organizes and maintains information: Organizes, processes, and maintains written or computerized records and other forms of information in a systematic fashion.

Interprets and communicates information: Selects and analyzes information and communicates the results to others using oral, written, graphic, pictorial, or multimedia methods.

Uses computers to process information: Employs computers to acquire, organize, analyze, and communicate information.

SYSTEMS

Understands systems: Knows how social, organizational, and technological systems work, and operates effectively within them.

Monitors and corrects performance: Distinguishes trends, predicts impact of actions on system operations, diagnoses deviations in the function of a system/organization, and takes necessary action to correct performance.

Improves and designs systems: Makes suggestions to modify existing systems to improve products or services, and develops new or alternative systems.

TECHNOLOGY

Selects technology: Judges which set of procedures, tools, or machines, including computers and their programs, will produce the desired results; helps others learn.

Applies technology to task: Understands the overall intent and the proper procedures for setting up and operating machines, including computers and their programming systems.

Maintains and troubleshoots technology: Prevents, identifies, or solves problems in machines, computers, and other technologies.

Source: Adapted from "The Secretary's Commission on Achieving Necessary Skills: What Work Requires of Schools: A SCANS Report for America 2000," U.S. Department of Labor, June 1991.

for the jobs of the future. Notice that this model distinguishes between performance skills and technical skills.

Competencies are here to stay. It is very likely that they are part of a permanent change in human resource management (Lawler and Ledford, 1997). In spite of their popularity, however, much confusion and misunderstanding concerning competencies remains. We will approach these issues as a series of challenges to be met during the installation of a competency system.

The Competency Challenge

Behavioral Technology® conducted a survey on the design and use of competency systems; 134 people in diverse organizations were queried. As shown in Exhibit 1.2, we found that the primary reason for introducing a competency system was to link interviews, appraisal, coaching, training, and compensation to vision, mission, values, and culture. Other reasons included planning for skills needed to grow the organization, communicating valued behaviors, and clarifying leadership focus. In short, competencies are expected to help managers and jobholders link, plan, communicate, and clarify.

The people we surveyed described problems with developing expensive competency models that were not broadly applied in their organizations. In addition, there were difficulties with using off-the-shelf competencies that did not accurately portray the uniqueness of their organizations or their jobs. Concerns about expense, acceptance, and legal defensibility can be added to the list.

Reviewing these survey findings is like looking at the Gulf of Mexico from our beach home. There are waves on the surface, but the real concern should be with the undercurrents that can take you out to sea and drown you. A competency system can be sunk if you don't consider the challenges associated with developing and installing it. These challenges are participation, measurement, negative feedback, job relatedness, and expense.

Exhibit 1.2. Survey Findings on the Objectives of Competency Systems.

Rank	Objectives
1.	Link interviews, appraisal, coaching, training, and compensation to vision, mission, values, and culture.
2.	Plan for the skills needed to grow the organization.
3.	Communicate valued behaviors.
4.	Clarify the focus of our leadership.
5.	Focus attention on quality/customer-oriented behaviors.
6.	Close skill gaps.
7.	Develop our competitive advantage.
8.	Identify selection criteria for interviews.
9.	Structure the topics discussed in a performance appraisal.
10.	Develop a 360° feedback system.
11.	Plan for succession.
12.	Orient managers to corporate strategy and culture.
13.	Encourage cross-functional cooperation.
14.	Guide promotional decisions.
15.	Ease the flow of people across business and global boundaries.

Challenge Number One: Participation

When it comes to competencies, there is a big conflict between *faster* and *better*. *Faster* contributes to efficiency, but it can ultimately turn out to be far more expensive and less effective. *Better* takes more time and broad participation. On average, it requires a year to develop and implement competencies (American Compensation Association, 1996).

Some would say that the critical factor is executive buy-in on competencies. Here I think of the executive retreat in which senior management uses competencies to define their organization's values and culture. A facilitator guides the discussion, makes notes on flip charts, and then does the write-up for approval. The resulting written statement then gives direction and clarity from the executive perspective. But the executive retreat that defines competencies without input from the rest of the organization may actually waste an opportunity. Broad participation is essential for acceptance and application.

This is not to say that the only value of participation is to get acceptance of new ideas. Participation is not a manipulative ploy—it is a mechanism for making your competencies more reflective of the true causes of performance. Here are some ways to use participation to improve the quality of the competencies you develop.

- Use a consultant to help executives develop a first draft of competencies for the organization. Through participation, members of the executive team are able to describe a new understanding of your competitive advantage in the marketplace.

- A leadership council is created that involves representatives from members of small business units. In a series of meetings they link HR to overall business planning and develop competencies that reflect the skills needed in the future.

- Over a nine-month period every person in the organization is given the opportunity to participate in developing the competency model. Their ideas are collected, edited for redundancy, checked for accuracy, and included in the model.

In the interest of saving time, one would think that having just a few representative groups do all of the competency development would be more efficient. Yet if you don't have broad involvement, you lose the opportunity to make the competency system "stick" with the people who will be using it. Competencies are more meaningful when a sizable percentage of people in your organization present opinions, think, fight, and write about them. Then you have an opportunity to build the commitment to actually use the system when it is rolled out.

Participation is a key to the successful installation of a competency system. During participation, behavioral language is used to link what needs to be done with individual actions. Competencies become the tools for direction and change. Competencies that are accepted become the elements of the language used in everyday communications. The result is the more specific expression of opinions, the expression of feelings behind facts, and the development of accurate performance measures.

Challenge Number Two: Measurement

How can we develop competencies that will hold up under pressure? When people don't get hired, promoted, or rewarded they ask hard questions, which can only be answered well by providing evidence for the reliability and validity of the measures used in decision making.

Detailed professional standards guide the procedures for conducting a study of the reliability and validity of any process that affects an individual's employment (Uniform Guidelines on Employee Selection Procedures, 1978; Society for Industrial and Organizational Psychology, 1987; American Educational Research Association, American Psychological Association, and National Council on Measurement in Education, 1985). The mastery of these standards typically involves graduate-level training in the behavioral sciences and working with a professional who has experience in this area. When properly applied, these standards guide the development of a measurement strategy to go along with your competencies.

Here is an example of a simple measurement strategy we used at a high-growth manufacturing operation needing many skilled knowledge workers. Candidates for key jobs were interviewed by me and members of management. After we each shared our initial ratings of each candidate, we systematically compared all of our

Measurement Standards Protect People from Junior Shrinks

Much of the energy for this book, and my passion for this topic, actually began in the mid-1970s when I was profiling participants of a seminar. After one class, a participant asked me to give him a test booklet, answer sheets, and scoring guidelines. I tactfully refused, explaining that to have access to this information he needed to place an order with the publishing house, accompanied by his educational credentials.

It became obvious that he did not have the qualifications to buy the test. However, as the conversation expanded, he said that he had "validated" the use of psychological tests in his own experience. He then showed me an unauthorized copy of a test profile and explained how he used an "intuitive" analysis to know who would be the best person for a job. He also pointed out that he had used the profile to assess a specific individual's suicidal tendencies. I was horrified to see the lack of professionalism, tact, or dignity used in assessing this person.

I was not able to change his thinking. He firmly believed that he could use a simple questionnaire to measure very complex personality characteristics and predict job performance effectively. To this day, I wish I had had another opportunity to coach him on how to gather meaningful, job-related information about a person at work and to use the information in a way that would enhance both performance and dignity. I hope that he will read this book and recognize the importance of effective measurement of and cautious inferences about people.

interview notes with the individual competencies being measured in the interviews. The match of notes to the competency was determined by a generic rating scale. This was the basis for the final interview ratings, which were then combined with other information to make decisions. After one of our sessions there was reasonable agreement on the candidates' skills for the job.

The next question related to validity. A test battery was developed that had been shown to be able to predict job performance. The development and installation of this system was a high-level professional task conducted by consultants who did this type of work exclusively. The result was a selection system that was based on evidence for reliable measurement and valid prediction. This was an ambitious task.

Challenge Number Three: Negative Feedback

A competency system that supports objective measurement can make some people feel insecure. Competencies are "hot"—they get a lot of attention—particularly when they affect selection, promotion, compensation, and career opportunities. An organization with enough courage to use competencies to measure performance with some degree of objectivity will experience conflict when some people don't earn good performance scores. But without courage, an organization's competencies may end up as a nice list of sayings that are posted on a bulletin board.

This is a challenge that reflects the conflicting forces in American culture involving the measurement of performance. For example, I heard President Clinton say that he would give a priority to measuring the educational proficiency of every student in the United States. He noted that many would disagree with this position. Achievement tests might lower the self-esteem of students who didn't do well. However, he continued by saying that accurate measurement is an important part of improving educational performance. This conflict over the value of educational measurement can be expected to continue for years.

There are similar conflicts over measurement of performance in the workplace. It is important to have accurate performance measurement when it influences compensation, promotion, and career opportunities. Many managers, however, don't want to broach negative information because they fear a legal battle stemming from a low rating. And talking to an individual about low performance on a competency measure may simply be unpleasant.

Some competency models present a competency with behavioral descriptors that do not allow for ratings of low performance. Others use a threshold of minimum acceptable performance in different jobs but give little opportunity to rate low, negative, or undesirable performance. These approaches may make the competency system more acceptable, but at the expense of leaving little room to describe negative performance.

A competency should be aligned with rating anchors that allow for ratings of high, average, and low performance. In particular, low ratings are valuable when they

- Identify why a person does not have minimum qualifications for a job
- Help a person recognize a performance problem
- Suggest needed training and learning experiences
- Describe the criteria for receiving no salary increase, being demoted, or losing one's job

Although negative information can be beneficial, it is often difficult to accept. Competency systems must face the challenge of introducing performance measurement that is both acceptable and representative.

Challenge Number Four: Job Relatedness

Using individual competencies to describe what a person is like as a person—intelligence, personality, values, skills, attitudes, and so forth—has an inherent appeal. This is what we attempt to do in everyday life.

Despite the common interest in understanding the whole person, there is the reality of the Americans with Disabilities Act of 1990 and the Civil Rights Act of 1991. These laws, and the emerging case law around them, require that any process that has an adverse impact on employment must be job related and consistent with business necessity (Civil Rights Act, 1991). Organizations have a responsibility to make job-related personnel decisions. Collecting "whole person" information can raise questions about the use of personal information when making these decisions.

Some firms are surprised by the practical application of this requirement, which is that the forms and procedures used in human resource applications should be related to specific jobs. An organization should have structured interviews that directly relate to the specific job under consideration. For example, Behavioral Technology and ADECCO (formerly ADIA), the temporary help firm, have been vendor and customer to one another for years. As part of this ongoing relationship, we developed a series of structured interviews specifically designed to select regional managers. Each of these interviews reflected the unique competencies required for doing that particular job well. For example, the competencies and questions developed for interviewing an office manager are different from those for interviewing a permanent placement specialist.

The need for job-related processes also applies to performance appraisal. A review of 295 circuit court decisions found that job analysis was one of several contributors to a favorable decision for the organization (Werner and Bolino, 1997). In addition, it was shown that issues related to fairness and due process contributed to the defensibility of an appraisal system.

Today, there is a particular challenge in developing job-related interviews and appraisal forms because jobs are changing so quickly.

Nonetheless, the requirement for defensibility has not changed. Competency systems that have an impact on employment should be job related.

Challenge Number Five: Expense

Development of competency-based interviews and appraisals for each job can be expensive. For example, an organization with one thousand associates could easily have eighty separate jobs. To have a job-related process, it is necessary to develop special interviews and appraisals for each of these jobs. It can be very expensive to develop and maintain eighty different structured interviews and appraisal forms.

Technology is being developed to address this competency challenge. At present there are several forms of cost-effective, computer-driven support for traditional HR processes. In recruiting, résumé scanning and the Internet are available, both of which get employers and candidates together more quickly. For interviewing, special-purpose job-analysis software creates job-related, structured interviews. For group problem solving, "groupware" enables individuals to participate in solving problems from different locations any time of the day. For performance appraisals, there are systems for writing appraisal observations and documentation. For coaching, there is a wide selection of computerized 360° feedback systems. For training, the Internet and company intranets will support just-in-time learning (learning information and skills just in time to solve work problems). For job evaluation, software is making the process of estimating the value of skills to an employer faster and better.

Competencies provide the mechanism for economically developing human resource applications such as structured interviews, performance discussion forms, goals for coaching, and instructional objectives. They are the link between what is sent from one application and received by another. This is one of the big reasons why job-related competencies will be around for some time.

Summary and Preview

The competency solution can reduce ambiguity and offer direction. It also enables an organization to link HR processes through competencies. However, the competency challenge requires consideration of how to get participation, develop reliable and valid measures, manage negative feedback, ensure job relatedness, and use technology to reduce expense.

In the next chapter we will explore the different meanings of *competencies* that are used in organizations and research. A distinction is made between the individual competencies discussed in this chapter and the core competencies, capabilities, values, and priorities that reflect an organization's identity.

2

Competencies, Capabilities, Values, Priorities, and Skills

Defining the Unique Characteristics of Your Organization and Its Associates

The beginning of wisdom is the definition of terms.
Socrates

A manager in a large organization once told me that they had used a very economical way to develop a competency-based HR system. They simply got a license to use the generic list of competencies that came in the materials of a training program that they had purchased. When I asked how they customized their competencies, he looked a little puzzled. But he rebounded quickly, saying that everyone agreed that the competencies were a valuable part of their 360° feedback system. He added that they were set up to use their competencies in other parts of their human resource system.

In all probability, this manager's list of competencies was an improvement over his organization's previous approach. But his competency system reminded me of my old truck when it was out of tune. It didn't matter how hard I pressed on the accelerator; I never got enough horsepower to carry a big load. The same applies to competencies. To get real benefits from your competencies, you have to "tune" them to your organization and its jobs.

The tuning of competencies to your needs involves taking advantage of the many different meanings that are associated with

Note: Thanks to Rob Most of MindGarden for his comments on this chapter.

21

them. In this chapter the *competency scope* expands on the definitions offered in Chapter One. It organizes the different ways that competencies can be used practically and addresses the different opportunities and pitfalls you will face as you customize them.

The Competency Scope

Competency concepts have become confusing because of the different ways the term *competency* is used by HR professionals and business strategists. It is not unusual to hear *core competency*, *capability*, *core value*, and *skill* used interchangeably. The competency scope will ensure that you know what I mean when I use these terms and, I hope, suggest some meanings with which we can all work.

As you will see, I limit the ways that I use the word *competency* and introduce some other terms to summarize other meanings in use. Please be sure that you understand these definitions before you finish this chapter, as they form the basic starting point for my prescription on linking HR applications in the following chapters.

The competency scope is a model that will help you target what needs to be done to meet the needs of your customers. It organizes important meanings around the word *competency* and then directs attention to your customers. This offers a perspective about competencies that moves you toward an external focus on what the customers need and away from an internal focus on what your organization is like. Although customer focus is not the topic of this book, it is worth mentioning that competencies without customers are not particularly meaningful. Competencies in service of customers are powerful business tools.

As you look at the scope (see Figure 2.1) you will see that two factors are essential for understanding the different ways that competencies are discussed. The *level* factor reflects how an organization can be effective in the marketplace, or how an individual can be effective in doing a particular job. The *type* factor distinguishes between the use of concepts such as technical knowledge and skills

Figure 2.1. The Competency Scope.

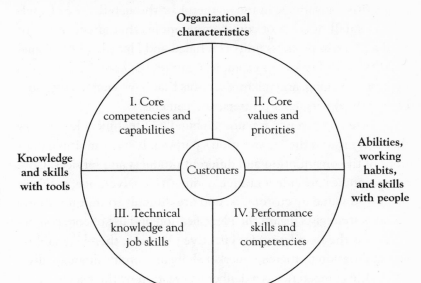

with tools, abilities, working habits, and skills with people. Later in this chapter, I'll discuss how both the level and the type factor relate to the KSAO model that is used in human resources (Harvey, 1991). Specifically, the model refers to K (knowledge), S (skill with tools), A (abilities) and O (other personal characteristics). Here, however, I discuss the four meanings that the combination of these factors suggests we consider when linking HR systems to the broad purpose of an organization.

Slice I: Core Competencies and Capabilities

The combination of knowledge and skills with tools is reflected at the organizational level in core competencies and capabilities (Lawler and Ledford, 1997). The term *core competency* was first used by C. K. Prahalad and Gary Hamel (1990) in what became one of the most requested reprints of the

Harvard Business Review. They argued that an organization gains a competitive advantage in the marketplace through the use of a relatively small number of core competencies that affect different products across business units (Prahalad and Hamel, 1990; Hamel and Prahalad, 1994). For example, Cannon has core competencies in optics, imaging, and microprocessors that have enabled it to succeed with copiers, laser printers, and cameras.

A core competency is a unique bundle of technical know-how that is central to the organization's purpose. It spans multiple divisions of the organization and different products and services. Core competencies provide a unique competitive advantage, result in perceived value by customers, and are difficult to imitate. Many business strategists regard the identification and use of core competencies as the foundation for effective planning, thereby enabling an organization to increase market share and profits dramatically.

A core competency is a deliberate creation by the executives of an organization. It requires a substantial commitment of time and resources to develop. But once in place, a core competency offers an organization a dramatic opportunity to outperform its competition.

A *capability* is also important to the organization's effectiveness and is perceived to be valuable by customers. It is a set of business processes strategically understood (Stalk, Evans, and Shulman, 1992). For example, Honda has been a strong competitor of General Motors not only because of its core competencies with engines and power trains but also because of its capability in deploying an effective dealer network (Hamel and Heene, 1994). In addition, Honda has an important capability in product development and introduction that enables it to bring products to market more quickly than the traditional product development cycle.

One expression of an organization's capabilities is through time-based competition (Lawler, 1996; Stalk and Hout, 1990). For example, CNN pioneered the delivery of news as it happens. This is not just a technical skill—it is a combination of business processes and capable management. Similarly, 10:30 A.M. delivery from Federal

Express reflects time-based competition, based on a powerful combination of people and work systems. However, as pointed out by Hamel and Prahalad (1994), speedy, on-time delivery from Federal Express is a benefit to the customer that is made possible by a core competency in logistics management.

Time-based competition combines capital resources with people skills. For example, Motorola has a plant that assembles cellular pagers within a few hours of receiving the order (Goldman, Nagel, and Preiss, 1995; Lawler, 1992). This speed reflects the combination of effective manufacturing technology with a committed workforce. Organizational capabilities and the skills of people are combined to form an "agile" organization that is focused on customer needs and is skilled in responding to them.

Far down the list of organizational capabilities would be the use of business skills that are important for any organization. For example, the application of generally accepted accounting principles to the creation of a financial report for shareholders is an important capability of a publicly traded organization. But it is a skill that is shared by all publicly traded companies.

Core competencies and capabilities are ideally expressed in a mission statement that specifically communicates what the organization will do for its customers. It should show the organization's purpose and suggest why it is different from all others in its area of enterprise. Instead of offering glowing promises, this mission statement should allude to how its core competencies and capabilities implement its purpose.

Slice II: Core Values and Priorities

Core values complement the technical aspects of work by explaining why the work is performed. There is a broad meaning behind this usage. At one level it encompasses shared beliefs of people in the organization and its culture, including norms on how to act. It is experienced as the "feel" of an organization—what it is really like to work there.

It is not easy to argue that a core value provides a *unique* competitive advantage to an organization. For example, a value for the dignity of the individual may distinguish some organizations from others. But this value is not necessarily unique. One can say, however, that a core value can provide a competitive advantage. For example, a case could be made that there was a time when culture-conscious Silicon Valley companies had a competitive advantage in recruiting. However, the claim of a *unique* advantage being provided by core values or an organizational culture is a stretch in comparison to the competitive advantage held by a company with new technologies and strong capabilities in using advanced work systems.

Priorities reflect an organization's emphasis on the use of individual competencies such as working habits and people skills to make business processes and work systems more efficient or effective. It is different from a capability that emphasizes the deployment of technical know-how, physical resources, or financial resources to improve performance. For example, organizational priorities on quality or innovation are very dependent on the human resources needed to carry them out (Pfeffer, 1994).

An important priority lies in an organization's willingness to use participation to improve performance and create a competitive advantage (Lawler, 1992). This priority is seen in the commitment to encourage associates to express their opinions on work issues. In addition, managers must be willing to listen to others' opinions, accept them when appropriate, and disagree when necessary. This bundle of people skills is very different from the core competencies and capabilities that objectively define a business strategy.

A question naturally arises about the point at which a business process that defines a capability differs from the people skills that define a priority. At least one part of the answer lies in the extent to which the process or system would see people as being interchangeable. When people are easily "plugged into" a business process, they are supporting an organizational capability. When a particular type of person with specific values and working habits is needed, we are probably dealing with an organizational priority.

A statement of core values and priorities describes how people actually do their work. It expresses the norms and boundaries of acceptable behavior and business practices. When expressed as a culture statement, it may go into the more symbolic aspects of the organization, including rituals, myths, and folklore. When expressed as a vision, it suggests ways to "see" how work will be done in the future.

Slice III: Technical Knowledge and Job Skills

Individuals use their technical knowledge and skills with tools to carry out their job responsibilities. These skills are typically learned in a formal learning situation and differ greatly across industries and jobs. For example, a software engineer takes classes that give her the knowledge to convert programs written in Visual Basic to C++. She is also skilled in working with software tools that make this conversion relatively easy. These skills were acquired through a combination of classroom instruction and practical experience with the languages.

Technical knowledge and job skills should be in support of the organization's core competencies and capabilities. Direct support might be seen when a technician for a chip manufacturer is able to use special photographic techniques to create extremely small circuits. Indirect support of technical competencies and capabilities is reflected in the word processing skills of the engineer who prepares a production report on chip production.

Technical skills training provides a logical way for an organization to maintain and extend its core competencies and capabilities. For example, a law firm with a capability in mergers and acquisitions would be wise to invest in providing training for new associates in this area. A software firm specializing in air traffic control systems would logically invest in training its associates on new Federal Aviation Administration regulations.

Slice IV: Performance Skills and Competencies

Performance skills and competencies include work habits, communication styles, leadership, and teamwork. They are easily transferred across different industries and jobs, and they reflect a person's efficiency or effectiveness in using technical knowledge and skills. For example, commitment to task is a performance skill that shows the extent to which a person will work hard to get results. This skill is important for a broad range of jobs that require self-direction and persistence. Remember that there are other examples of performance skills in the competency model presented in Chapter One.

Performance skills should be used not only in doing a job but also in support of the core values and priorities of the organization in which a person works. These skills and competencies will vary from organization to organization. A communication style that is respectful and tactful may reflect a values statement of one organization, whereas a domineering and aggressive style may support the values of another organization.

A performance skill can be directly observed and described at a behavioral level. It can be described in terms of what a person is observed to say or do. In contrast, a competency involves an inference about what a person is like. Competencies include constructs such as intelligence and personality. Exhibit 2.1 gives examples.

Historically, *competency* has been used to refer to individual characteristics. However, I prefer using the word *skills* over competencies when referring to individual characteristics used to do a job (Harvey, 1991). To some extent this is because I want to make a distinction between individual characteristics and what business strategists talk about as core competencies. But more important, I feel that most HR systems should deal practically with the skills that a person can be observed to use at work.

Although the competency scope includes both abilities and personality, the perspective offered in this book minimizes the role of these elements in linking HR systems. An emphasis on skills makes it relatively easy for a manager to determine the extent to which a skill is used or not used at work. It is much more difficult, however, for an associate to do a competency assessment involving abilities or personality. Grounding HR systems in skill descriptions is more effective because such descriptions can be reliably used by most people at work.

Behavioral language can create a link between the organizational characteristics in slice I and slice II and the individual characteristics in slice III and slice IV. Before attending to this challenge, let's explore some practical examples of the distinct meanings of organizational characteristics and individual skills.

Exhibit 2.1. A Contrast of a Core Competency and a Performance Skill.

There is a big difference between a core competency used in developing a business strategy and a performance skill. For example, here is a performance skill involving policy and procedures:

> Follows procedures: Conforms to prescribed policies and procedures, even when it is inconvenient to do so; encourages others to follow procedures; tells others how policies and procedures enhance or constrain performance; explains to management how policies and procedures may interfere with productivity.

In contrast, a core competency is a unique bundle of technical skills that contribute to the organizations success in its marketplace. Here is an example of a core competency for an electronics manufacturer in the early 1990s.

> Telephonic miniaturization: Reduce the space required for telephone circuitry continuously while expanding functions; introduce miniaturized cellular-phone components before competitors; show annual improvement on the time-to-market for new products; innovate manufacturing technologies to provide highly reliable cellular phone components.

Notice that this core competency reflects the combined use of technical knowledge and skills with tools and equipment. In addition, it has exceptional value in the marketplace when it is unique. Then the organization has a competitive advantage over other organizations with similar products or services.

Organizational Characteristics

When combined, slices I and II reflect the organization's identity, including the broad work context in which an individual is to perform. The more familiar components of organizational identity include vision, mission, values, and culture. Roughly, I would expect vision and mission to reflect core competencies and capabilities. Core values and priorities would be reflected in a values statement and shared working habits.

One example of the relationship between a core competency and identity comes from a conversation between Sam Walton, the founder of Wal-Mart, and Fred Smith, the founder of Federal Express. Walton said that many people believed Wal-Mart was successful because it placed big stores in small towns. He said that the real key to the company's success, however, was that it learned to substitute information for inventory (Wetherbe, 1996). The perceived identity of the organization feels real to its customers, yet the essential identity is in its core competencies.

Wal-Mart developed a core competency around information and inventory management. Each cash register was linked to a satellite to send sales information to a distribution center. Shipments were quickly sorted across loading docks to replace the inventory before the next work day. When introduced, this core competency was unique in retailing, and it gave Wal-Mart a strong competitive advantage (Stalk, Evans, and Shulman, 1992).

Core competencies provide the basis for an organization to define itself beyond its specific end products. Sony was one of the first companies to apply solid-state electronics to AM radios. But the long-term value of this application was not the sale of radios but the sale of televisions, recorders, compact disc players, and a variety of other products (Hamel and Prahalad, 1994). One core competency made several products possible and better.

The same is true of Honda. In the late 1960s, I rode a silver Honda motorcycle that was just as exciting as the hippie movement and the music of the time. It was Honda's core competencies relating to engines and power trains, however, not its original motorcycle, that determined the company's future. Honda used those core competencies and capabilities to leverage itself into new products, such as cars, mowers, tractors, engines, and generators (Hamel and Prahalad, 1994; Stalk, Evans, and Shulman, 1992).

Core values and priorities are quite different from core competencies, as demonstrated in a values implementation project at Fairview Hospital and Healthcare Services in Minneapolis, Minnesota (Norling and Pashley, 1995). Fairview sought to identify and strengthen the core values of the organization so as to develop a sense of community, which would lead to greater trust and organizational commitment. Fairview made a sustained and systematic effort, over a three-year period, to reinforce the behaviors that reflect the core values of the organization.

The project began with the creation of a Values Identification Task Force, which used broad participation with representative groups in the organization over a fifteen-month period. The original draft of thirteen values was refined by senior managers and eleven focus groups containing ninety-nine employees. Altogether, the project involved about three hundred individuals in over nine hundred hours of discussion. As a result, the values were clarified to reflect the Lutheran heritage of the organization and the spiritual dimension of their values. For example, the core values of the organization included compassion, dignity, integrity, and service.

The values of the organization were communicated through meetings, video, and newsletter articles. Training classes were designed to include discussion of values dilemmas, a strengthening exercise, and new employee orientation. Projected changes in human resource systems included the design of a personal development planning system, questions for selection interviews, and values surveys.

Lessons from implementation suggest that the strengthening of core values was a powerful way to make the organization more

effective, regardless of the extent to which they reflect the organization's vision. Also, the statement of core values legitimized discussion of important issues. Difficult topics were easier to bring up
when they related to core values.

Individual Characteristics

Slices III and IV pertain to the skills used by individuals
to perform their specific jobs. They reflect the job content, including specific tasks to be performed, and the individual characteristics needed to carry them out. These are very different from the
organization's identity and the context of the work.

Slices III and IV represent the historical emphasis on individual skills in human resources. The importance of technical job skills
is documented in the extensive listing of jobs and job tasks in the
Dictionary of Occupational Titles. Performance skills are represented
in the testing movement that emerged following World War II.
Standardized tests were used to assess intelligence, personality, and
patterns of behavior. The emergence of assessment centers in the
1960s offered "assessment dimensions," which are job-related,
behavior-based selection standards. Assessors rated candidates' performance on the dimensions based on their performance of various
tasks and exercises. Individual assessments, involving testing and
interviewing by an industrial psychologist, also emerged as a very
specialized process for determining the performance skills of managers and key workers.

In addition to being an HR tool, assessment technology offers a
perspective that distinguishes between a performance skill and a competency. The behavioral approach to assessment would say that a
performance skill can be directly observed and described in terms
of the things a person is observed to say or do. Here, performance
skills are measured by interviews, assessment centers, or simulations.

The psychometric approach says that in addition to the measures used with the behavioral approach, a competency can be
measured by personality and cognitive ability tests. Here, a compe-

tency involves more of an inference about what a person is like than a description of what the person does. With this approach a competency is a construct that is not seen but is believed to exist because of the logic behind a test or another type of measure.

The pure competency approach is different from the psychometric approach in its statement of what a competency is not. Advocates of this approach trace their thinking to an article written by David McClelland, a Harvard psychologist who argued against the use of intelligence and aptitude tests (McClelland, 1973; Spencer and Spencer, 1993). Instead, he said that intelligence testing should be replaced by competency-based testing. Although many of McClelland's assertions about testing have been questioned (Barrett and Depinet, 1991), he did energize research on individual characteristics that would influence job performance.

The scope model does not accommodate the pure competency approach because of its rejection of cognitive ability under its definition. The competency scope does, however, align with both the behavioral approach and the psychometric approach. The practical value of this relationship is that it describes a linkage between the competency scope to KSAs or, to use the more current term, KSAOs (Harvey, 1991). Consequently, we can relate organizational identity, core competencies and capabilities, and core values and priorities to the common denominator of all forms of HR assessment.

Recall that the KSAO model (see Exhibit 2.2) is used in HR to describe and organize the individual characteristics needed to do a job well. Furthermore, the elements of the KSAO model currently used in HR can be reflected in skill definitions. Here is a skill definition for a service representative containing phrases that link to KSAOs.

Customer contact: Able to apply *knowledge* of customer-contact procedures and service guidelines to customer needs; uses *skills* with word processing and fax transmission in customer communications; demonstrates *ability* to comprehend the technical nature of customer problems; uses *other* skills in coping and

Exhibit 2.2. The KSAO Model.

Knowledge—the specific information necessary to perform the tasks of a job. This is typically acquired through formal education, on-the-job-training, and work experience.

Skill—proficiency in using tools and equipment on the job. This skill may be acquired in an educational environment or be learned on the job in an informal way. Some examples of skill with tools include using an arc welder, typing with a word processor, or driving heavy equipment.

Ability—concepts such as intelligence, spatial orientation, reaction time, and stamina. Abilities are often measured by tests that provide estimates of the extent to which the person has the specific ability needed to perform a job task.

Other—additional characteristics needed for doing a job well. This category includes performance skills, attitudes, personality, and other personal characteristics required of the jobholder. For example, coping or creativity are "other" characteristics, reflecting how a person does a job rather than what was done on the job.

---

communicates by restating a problem and expressing a personal responsibility for solving it.

Another way to organize these concepts is to break the KSAO model into two factors: (1) the K and S conveniently organize into technical/job skills; (2) the A and O translate into performance skills.

K and S at the Organizational and Individual Levels

The competency scope suggests a comprehensive way to align with the KSAO model. Core competencies and capabilities and technical/job skills (slices I and III) reflect the K and the S components of the KSAO model. At the organizational level, core competencies and capabilities are the shared technical knowledge (K) and skill with tools (S) that are used by the organization to compete and survive in the marketplace. For example, flat screen technology is a type of shared knowledge that will provide an important capability for some electronics firms in the future. At the individual level, however, the emphasis is on one person's use of the knowledge. For example, an engineer may be expected to have technical knowledge about the gases used in producing high-resolution flat screens for computer monitors.

Core values and priorities, along with performance skills, constitute the A and the O of the KSAO model (slices II and IV). For example, *ability* is found in the learning organization that is adept in acquiring new skills (Senge, 1990). At the same time *other* characteristics, such as a shift of mind, are needed to understand how organizational systems cause work outcomes. Another *other* characteristic would include a strong work ethic at the organizational level—an important habit for associates to share when many of them will spend the long hours at work needed to give customers quality.

At the individual level (slice IV) the competency scope accounts for abilities such as the ability to remember spoken instructions. Assessment of a firefighter's explosive strength is another type of ability that is included here.

A Practical Dilemma

The linkage of HR applications to an organization's identity, core competencies and capabilities, core vision, and priorities is best achieved through an emphasis on the behavioral approach. The price to pay here is significant. We lose the elegance of ideas and volumes of research on ability and personality assessment. For example, not using abilities to link HR applications does not take full advantage of an abilities-oriented competency model (Fleishman and Reilly, 1992). Ability measures were also used in assessing students' learning needs to introduce effective changes in an MBA program (Boyatzis, Cowen, and Kolb, 1995). However, these types of measures are the domain of the expert in psychometrics. They are not the best choice for linking HR systems to the organization's identity because few people are qualified to use them.

Personality is another O characteristic. There is substantial evidence that personality tests can predict job performance (Barrick and Mount, 1991; Tett, Jackson, and Rothstein, 1991). Personality assessment, however, requires more training than is typically afforded line managers. Like ability testing, personality testing that affects a person's employment cannot be easily applied at all levels of an organization. A behavioral approach that emphasizes the description of actions more than the assessment of personal qualities is the more likely tool for linking HR applications.

It is important to be able to relate KSAOs logically to core competencies, capabilities, core values, and priorities. This enables you to use a language that is consistent with the terminology currently used in human resources, thereby providing a linkage with existing HR procedures and research. It is practical to be cautious, however, about using abilities and personality as part of a competency model to link HR systems. Instead, convert A and O concepts to performance skills that are expressed in behavioral language.

There is an additional limitation on the use of performance skills as part of a competency model. For example, it would seem logical to develop a list of ten to twelve organizational competencies and then interview job candidates on their "fit" to the organization. Similarly, you could develop a 360° process in which all associates received feedback on the organization's competencies. However, there is a problem with this thinking: It involves employment law.

The assessment of individual skills differs from the use of organizational competencies in a very important way. Skills assessment must conform to the requirements of the Civil Rights Act of 1991 and the Americans with Disabilities Act. Arguably, core competencies, capabilities, values, and priorities define your organization's strategic position. But the HR systems for your organization *must* be based on individual jobs and *should* reflect organizational strategy. To develop your HR system based strictly on core values and corporate culture is to ignore more than thirty years of case law on employment.

> **HR competency systems must be job related and should reflect core competencies, capabilities, core values, and priorities.**

You will see later that it is possible tó have a job-related process that reflects both the content of the job through individual skills and the context of the job through organizational competencies, capabilities, values, and priorities. This is achieved by developing job-related competencies to reflect both the context of work offered by an organization and the content of a job held by an individual.

Summary and Preview

The terms *competency, capability,* and *skill* are used in many ways. At a broad level their meanings reflect organizational characteristics, including core competencies and capabilities, as well as core values and priorities. At an individual level they reflect individual skills, which include technical knowledge and job skills with tools, and performance skills, which include other characteristics such as leadership and organization.

Some competencies, capabilities, values, and priorities are strategic, that is, they are related to gaining a competitive advantage in the marketplace. In contrast, individual skills are used for specific applications such as interviewing, appraising, coaching, and training.

In the next chapter we will discuss *operationalizing* performance skills. This approach will enable you to use behavioral observation, description, and inference to communicate clearly what a person needs to do to do a job well.

3

Operationalizing Performance Skills

Using Behavioral Language to Turn Vague Characteristics into Observable Actions

If you only have a hammer, everything looks like a nail.

Anonymous

A new client retained our consulting group to review his company's performance skills. "We want to use our model to assess individuals throughout the organization," he said. "Our system needs to cover everything from coping to leadership."

We scheduled a consulting day for this purpose. At the client's offices, I was allowed to see a notebook of detailed descriptions concerning the characteristics of people regarded as desirable for the organization. At first glance, the characteristics seemed to be comprehensive and meaningful, and each performance skill was accompanied by descriptions of the actions that a person would take. So far, so good.

The problems began to emerge as I carefully read through the performance skills. Many of the words were consistent with the organization's culture statement, but their meanings were not clear. Even though there was an attempt to describe desired actions, the descriptions were not written in behavioral language.

Here is a simulated example of one of the performance skills and action statements associated with it.

Concern for customer service: Is aware of the different types of needs of internal and external customers; has a strong desire to be of service to others; uses interpersonal understanding to conceptualize customer problems; has empathy for the customer; finds enjoyment in serving others with a smile.

Actions to look for: (1) Shows courtesy when responding to customer requests; (2) is willing to "partner" with customers in problem solving; (3) demonstrates a full understanding of customer needs; (4) is willing to be a resource for internal customers; (5) is sensitive to the unstated needs of the customers.

After reading just one performance skill the problem was obvious. The company had spent a great deal of time and energy in developing their competency model, but using the information for selection interviews, appraisal, coaching, and training wasn't easy. Their statement was full of words whose meanings were unclear, such as *concern, aware, desire, understanding, conceptualize, empathy, enjoyment, partner, willing,* and *sensitive.* The words did not describe the actions to be taken when using the skill. So we rewrote the competencies in a way that emphasized specific actions rather than vague characteristics. For example, "Has a strong desire to be of service to others" was rephrased as, "Asks customers, 'How may I be of service to you?'"

This client ultimately had a positive outcome. Along the way, though, he experienced a lot of disappointment and misunderstanding because he did not invest the time to operationalize competencies as they were being developed.

What Is an Operational Definition?

An *operational definition* explains a concept by describing the steps that need to be taken to observe it. It is a technique that was first developed in physics but was later adopted for psychology as a method for defining abstract concepts. This approach can be used to define performance skills and show exactly what can be seen or heard when the competency is being used.

> **Operationalizing a competency means that you convert a phrase like "believes in the dignity of the worker" to a series of statements like "restates concerns accurately" and "suggests ways to communicate about sensitive matters." This approach describes the *actions* of a person who believes in the dignity of the worker.**

Some of the confusion about individual skills and competencies stems from interchanging the term *competency* with terms such as *dimension, skill definition, skill dimension, success factor, attribute, intervening variable, hypothetical construct, KSAO,* and *human factor.* In addition, performance skills and competencies may be defined with statistical techniques, such as factor analysis, to clarify the basic ingredients of performance.

The word *excellence* offers a good example of the problems associated with defining a performance skill. What does *excellence* mean to you? What does it mean to others in your organization? What does it mean to a low-performing team? What does it mean in a performance discussion? The only effective way for your organization to answer these questions is systematically to observe people doing something with excellence and describe it. Continue observing and describing until you have a reasonably complete description of the actions that are taken when excellence is observed.

It is not likely that you can do a good job of operationally defining performance skills all by yourself. You will need to involve other people to develop a rich, accurate description. For example, this is how I once worded a performance skill before I got help.

Manages conflict: Able to express opinions directly and clearly without abuse or manipulation; listens to the opinions and feelings of others and demonstrates understanding by restatement;

communicates disagreement to persons in authority as necessary; asks for negative feedback in order to learn.

I showed my definition to a colleague and asked a simple question: "What steps would I need to take to see or hear someone managing conflict?"

"Be in the conference room at three this afternoon," he whispered, anticipating a heated meeting coming up later in the day.

I asked, "What will you see or hear in this meeting that relates to my skill definition?"

After a pause, he said, "I would begin by looking for the things that are already stated in the definition." He wrote on a flip chart:

Expresses opinions directly (Yes or No)

Restates others' comments (Yes or No)

Disagrees to make a point (Yes or No)

Asks for negative feedback (Yes or No)

Then he said, "I would drop the reference to 'manipulation.'" He scratched the word out. "Nobody will know what that means. . . . Also, you forgot to include the idea of making suggestions that will resolve disagreements." After some discussion we added this statement: "Suggests a compromise in order to advance work."

Of course, this brief meeting was not enough. To be useful the performance skill still needed a lot of work. Nonetheless, the example shows the importance of involving others when defining performance skills. Participation enables you to develop a more complete description of the actions that define the skill. The people in your organization can then agree on what to look for when they are using it.

Behavioral Language and Performance Skills

Behavioral language is very concrete. It describes what you can see or hear being done. When necessary, you can use operational definitions to define the steps to take if you want to know where or how to observe a competency being used. However, for practical purposes, behavioral language can be used to ensure understanding, leaving operational definitions for creating precise definitions that meet scientific standards.

A behavior is an action that you can observe, describe, and verify.

A *performance skill* is written in behavioral language. It indicates the actions needed to do a job well, organizes job tasks, provides direction, and serves as a measurement standard. It is robust because the actions used to describe a performance skill can be reliably described through the written or spoken word. This means that another person should be able to verify that the description is reasonably accurate. This is the natural result of involving others in describing what people do when they are using the performance skill.

Verification shows the extent to which two or more people agree on a behavioral description.

A performance skill is more concrete than personality traits, abilities, or motivations. We can recognize that these attributes are important characteristics of people at work. However, special training is required to be skilled in using these types of concepts practically. A competency system that is based on personality traits uses words that potentially send different messages to different people.

The tangible nature of a performance skill means that it helps reduce the influence of biases, stereotypes, and snap judgments on people. It is especially valuable in helping managers reduce their subjectivity in decision making. The focus is on making reasonable inferences about people, based on verifiable information.

A practical way to write a behavioral performance skill is to use the phrase *able to* when you start the definition. Then continue with an action verb that shows what the person does when using the skill (see Exhibit 3.1, which contrasts trait-based competencies with behavior-based performance skills). I prefer to separate each phrase with a semicolon and group them all together so they can be conveniently placed at the top of a page. This leaves room for things like interview questions, tasks for performance discussion, coaching goals, and instructional objectives.

Trait-based competencies are inferences about internal characteristics rather than descriptions of what is said or done. Exhibit 3.2 tests the degree to which competency statements are behavior based or trait based. Of course, it is natural to draw conclusions about people, but it is preferable to anchor your conclusions with descriptions of the actions that are taken rather than with perceptions or general impressions.

Exhibit 3.1. A Contrast of Trait-Based Competencies and Behavior-Based Performance Skills.

Trait-Based	*Behavior-Based*
Ego strength: Has abilities such as internal courage and fortitude; exhibits strength when most people retreat; thinks in a balanced way; keeps business goals in perspective.	Coping: Able to maintain problem-solving speech and actions while responding to interpersonal conflict, hazardous conditions, personal rejection, hostility, or time demands.
Initiative: Is a self-starter; motivated to get exceptional results; willing to put extra effort into doing the job; thinks about ways to improve results.	Commitment to task: Able to start and persist with specific courses of action until an objective is reached; spends long hours at work; makes a personal sacrifice to reach goals.
Values: Ability to think in ways that reflect strong values; believes in traditional values such as family and hard work; possesses an attitude that "honesty is the best policy."	Integrity: Follows written guidelines on business ethics; explains the core business values to associates in a complete manner; corrects others on conforming to the statement of shared values and procedures.

Exhibit 3.2. Self-Test.

Rank the following competency statements in order, based on the degree to which they are behavior based or attribute based. Start by placing a *1* next to the behavior-based statement that is most specific. Continue until you have assigned the highest number to the attribute-based statement that is most abstract. The answers are at the bottom.

Rank	Competency
_____	Focus on results: Able to persist on projects/assignments until completion; talks about tasks to be done; asks questions about ways to get results; points out work that is not up to expectation.
_____	Focus on results: Has a strong ability to get results; is motivated to show excellence in all aspects of life; has a high interest in reaching objectives; shows up whenever work is to be done.
_____	Focus on results: Has a high activity level as measured by physical movement; content analysis of speech reflects high reference to tasks; measures of blood pressure, heart rate, and adrenal corticoids reflect a strong physical energy level.
_____	Focus on results: Is a self-starter; has qualities such as drive and eagerness; thinks about new ways to get results; wants to get results and be successful; has a positive attitude about paying the price to get ahead.

Answers: The correct sequence from top to bottom is 2, 3, 1, 4. I probably surprised you with the molecular description of "physical movement" and "blood pressure." Even though this type of description is rare at work, it is nonetheless the most specific.

Traits often become labels that seem to stick to people even after they have changed. For example, someone who was labeled a "slacker" on projects six months ago may have improved that trait with concentrated effort. Behavioral language helps you to notice the change as you draw new inferences about the person.

People at all educational levels in an organization can effectively use behavior-based performance skills. Behavioral wording makes expectations and performance criteria very clear. As a result, job-holders have a good understanding of what needs to be done on the job, as well as a sense of fairness about how performance is to be evaluated.

The use of performance skills in the selection interview makes this point very nicely. Each interviewer asks preplanned questions that are organized under several performance skills. Each skill definition reflects the strategic initiatives of the organization and the requirements of specific jobs. Each question is designed to help candidates provide information about their skills for the job. The candidates' responses are evaluated by comparing their answers with the performance skills.

Occasionally, performance skills are stated in an extremely specific way that describes a very small action or physical response. For example, the movement of one facial muscle is a molecular behavior that may be important in describing an actor's smile. However, in most cases, it is OK to talk about a smile, just like it makes sense to talk about walking without describing the precise movements of the ligaments in the left foot. You can be reasonably general in your descriptions as long as people reliably know what you mean.

Performance Skills Support Objectivity

A performance skill is written in a way that invites objective comparison of what was done to a description of what needs to be done. For example, in today's environment it is important for a salesperson to be able to assess and manage the political influences on decision makers. This suggests that an important skill for the job might be defined as "reading the system." This skill definition then becomes part of the salesperson's regular debriefing with a sales manager on account status. A comparison of what was done with the account with the skill definition then can provide an objective basis for performance management.

A large-scale project to revise the *Dictionary of Occupational Titles* was undertaken by the Utah Department of Employment Security (Peterson and others, 1995). Exhibit 3.3 provides an

Exhibit 3.3. An Individual Competency with Rating Guidelines.

Making decisions and solving problems: Combining, evaluating, and reasoning with information and data. These processes involve making decisions about the relative importance of information and choosing the best solution.

Level

What level of this activity is needed to perform this job?

Reaching conclusions after considering a large number of choices that are often ambitious or abstract, where there are competing viewpoints and alternatives that must be considered before reaching final decisions, and the solutions decided upon will have very significant impact.	7
	Making the final decisions about a company's five-year strategic
	6 plan.
	Determining the best way to perform brain surgery.
	5
	4 Deciding how to settle a moderate-sized insurance claim. Selecting the location for a major department store.
	3
Reaching conclusions after considering a few choices that are usually well defined, where there are a limited number of possible actions, and the decisions or solutions will have minor impact.	2 Routing truck deliveries. Determining the meal selection
	1 for a cafeteria.
	NR Not relevant at all for performance on this job.

Note: Reproduced from Peterson and others, 1995. Copyright © 1995, Utah Department of Employment Security (now part of the Department of Workforce Services). Used with permission.

example of how they used behavioral language to describe activities important for job success. As you can see, the competency is aligned with a behaviorally anchored rating scale; descriptors make ratings relatively easy and reliable.

Performance skills and descriptive rating scales are the foundation of the behavioral approach in objective decision making. The three steps of the behavioral approach are as follows:

Step 1: Observe what a person says or does. This seems like the obvious beginning to most interactions. What is not obvious, however, is that this step limits you to observing. Expansion of the observation into a snap judgment is not allowed. This step requires that you just observe—nothing more.

Step 2: Describe what you observe in relation to the performance skill. You can do this in writing, but sometimes it makes sense simply to describe your observation silently to yourself. The real test of the second step is whether another person can verify what you described. Make your description as factual as possible, regardless of how you feel about what you saw or heard.

Step 3: Infer from your description. If you have a rating scale, use it. If not, you can still go beyond the words used to describe what you observed. You may draw conclusions, make predictions, or develop a hypothesis about the other person. The rule of thumb is that this expansion of your description should be reasonable in light of what you observed and described.

You can evaluate your inference, prediction, or hypothesis by making new observations to confirm or challenge it.

Steps of the Behavioral Approach
1. Observe   2. Describe   3. Infer

If you are like most people, your perceptions of a person are influenced by your reactions—that is, how you feel about the person. But with the behavioral approach, perception is not reality. The three steps of the behavioral approach enable you to develop a reasonable understanding of another person by substituting observation, description, and inference for perception.

A robust performance skill supports the steps of the behavioral approach. It will not contain abstract words and references to traits, motivations, cognitions, and patterns of thought. By using words that describe behavior, you can be very clear about what you mean.

If more people were skilled in using behavior-based performance skills, there would be less prejudice in the world. Through stereotyping, one person is assumed to be like the perception of a whole group of people. This interferes with recognizing the great differences among the individuals in a group.

Summary and Preview

A great challenge at work is to communicate with descriptive words while being cautious about your inferences about people. Focus on actions, not your gut feelings or intuitions. Performance skills aid in this process because they suggest what to observe and how to describe it. They provide a standard as you expand your interpretations in a reasonable way.

In the next chapter we will explore how the identity of an organization can become the target for alignment. We'll also discuss how an organization's identity can be reflected in and reinforced by interviews, appraisal, coaching, and training.

4

Achieving Structural Alignment

Supporting Organizational Identity with Human Resource Systems

The main thing is to keep the main thing the
main thing.

Jim Barksdale, CEO of Netscape

I once owned a car that seemed to stay out of alignment. It drove as though the front wheels were trying to go in different directions. It would begin to shudder when I drove over forty miles an hour. Needless to say, this made me very cautious as I drove, plus the ride was not very comfortable. The car's being out of alignment caused anxiety, low performance, and discomfort.

One of the major challenges facing organizations today involves alignment—that is, getting everyone committed to move in the same direction. A clear understanding of the direction in which the organization is headed helps people direct themselves at every level and in every job (Labovitz and Rosansky, 1997).

Organizations attempt to get alignment in numerous ways. Some are effective and others are just window dressing. One effective approach is to help individuals see how their personal goals overlap with the goals of the organization. This is *personal alignment*. It is achieved through participation and open discussion.

Our firm was once engaged to help an advertising agency develop the personal alignment of its key associates with plans to redirect the organization. A working weekend out of town was set aside for executives, managers, and associates from all of the agency's divisions. Prior to the meeting, I asked everyone to formulate a question about the identity of the agency that they couldn't answer. These questions were to relate to what the agency was, where it was going, and how individuals fit into the scheme. During the meeting the questions were drawn from a box and read aloud. The group discussed each until they formed a conclusion. They wrote the conclusions on a flip chart and returned to them as needed.

On the following day, we summarized all of the points that were covered. Distilling the predominant ideas, we wrote the one paragraph that became the agency's mission statement.

Because the associates had been able to define how the organization was important to them, the agency experienced a surge in performance after the meeting. The meeting had provided a high level of participation about the identity of the agency and had aligned individual motivations with its goals. As a result, the agency increased its client list meaningfully.

Another type of alignment can be developed by using behavioral language to link HR systems to an organization's identity, including its core competencies and capabilities, values, and priorities. This is what I call *structural alignment*. It uses the systems, procedures, and forms of the HR effort to reinforce and communicate how the individual fits into the big picture. Through structural alignment, the words and phrases of the organization's vision, mission, values, and culture can become a part of selection, appraisal, coaching, and training.

Structural alignment can be carried out only when there is a clear description of the identity of the organization. The process is made easier when the organization's identity is expressed in behavioral language. Behavioral language offers a clearer target for aligning human resource systems with the direction of the organization.

Would associates in your organization run the risk of rewording an identity statement that feels good to the executives who wrote it? If not, there probably was not enough participation to make the statement a shared point of reference.

Organizational Identity: The Target for Alignment

An organization's identity is reflected in the core competencies and capabilities and in the core values and priorities described in the competency scope. Here is a brief refresher from Chapter Two.

Core Competencies and Capabilities; Core Values and Priorities

A *core competency* is a unique bundle of technical knowledge and skills that provides an organization with a competitive advantage in its marketplace. A *capability* includes the sound business processes and their professional management that enable an organization to do its work effectively.

A *core value* describes the norms and boundaries that are used to guide and evaluate how a person acts. A *priority* describes shared work habits that emphasize a way to get results. Priorities often place an emphasis on the performance skills associated with quality, work systems, and participation.

Core competencies, capabilities, core values, and priorities all operate at the same time. For example, a hypothetical company specializing in family photography develops core competencies with lasers, computer imaging, and digital carving equipment to produce family sculptures and murals as new products. This bundle of technical knowledge and skills enables the company to be a unique studio.

The capabilities of this organization would include rapid delivery, materials management, and programming. In addition, the organization would need to apply the correct accounting techniques and have skill in marketing the products. When combined, the core competencies and capabilities would be reflected in a mission statement describing the purpose of the organization.

The core values would be seen in the original vision of the founders—that is, help families see their loved ones in three dimensions. The values and culture of the organization might include expectations regarding clean, nonsexist language and a commitment for performance-based compensation.

A priority might be reflected in the quality of the sculptures. Each image is presented in exact detail and hand polished. Associates use self-discipline and well-defined work systems to ensure that each sculpture is a work of art. These core values and priorities are reflected in a statement of vision, values, or culture.

The *identity* of an organization is a critical target for creating a structural alignment of HR systems. This is achieved by expressing an identity statement in behavioral language and then using it in the forms and procedures prevalent in human resources. Matching the words and meanings of the identity statement with the words and meanings used in human resources provides an opportunity to emphasize continuously what actions are important for individuals to take.

Virtue-Based and Behavior-Based Identity

Statements of vision, mission, values, and culture often use language that portrays the organization as having the qualities or attributes that are typically considered desirable in individuals. For example, a virtue-based identity statement would include terms such as *integrity, innovative,* and *creative.* Yet if these words are not defined behaviorally, associates won't reliably know how to take the actions that are consistent with the identity statement. Exhibit 4.1 is an exercise in converting identity statements into behavioral language.

A behavior-based identity statement describes what a person needs to do to be in alignment with the organization's vision, mission, values, and culture. An identity statement worded in behav-

Exhibit 4.1. Clarify Identity with Behavioral Language.

Convert these phrases from mission statements into behavioral language.

Identity Phrase	Behavioral Language
The world's premier provider of	
Distinctive and successful in all that we do	
Passion for innovation	
Dedicated to quality	
Better than the best	
Known for our teamwork	
Faithful to our core values and beliefs	
Recognized as the best in our industry	
World class in all that we do	
Innovative, aggressive, ethical, and successful	

ioral language emphasizes actions and outcomes over catchy phrases and personal qualities.

The Mission Statement Book (Abrahams, 1995) provides many examples of the differences between virtue-based identity and behavior-based identity. The virtue-based statements abound with glowing phrases and advertising copy but fail to describe the organization in terms of what people really do. The behavior-based statements offer clear descriptions of the actions people take that reflect the organization's identity.

A virtue-based identity statement may have supporting information that converts the virtues into actions to take. In this case, the virtue provides a general meaning that works for the audience for which it was written. But the internal audience for the statement needs to see what is really meant by the virtues (Whiteley and Hessan, 1996).

Behavioral language can be used with each of the components of an identity statement. An organization's vision, mission, values, and culture can be described as individual actions to be taken rather than desirable qualities and attributes. This enables an identity statement to describe where you are going, what you are going to do, how to act along the way, and the skills you will use in getting there.

The traditional way of stating identity through vision, mission, and values does not exactly parallel my definitions of core competencies, capabilities, core values, and priorities. A case could be made that mission should reflect core competencies and capabilities as well as priorities. Vision could be expected to align with core values and priorities. However, this shoe is too tight. The alignment between organizational characteristics and a statement of identity needs to be loose enough to allow for the creative description of identity in light of how the organization really operates.

A Behavior-Based Vision

A behavior-based vision statement is a word picture that describes a future setting for work and the actions that associates will take in it. It helps associates imagine, and possibly experience, the long-range goals of the organization. It puts the future of the organization in everyone's mind's eye (Nanus, 1992).

With this approach, you would express a vision statement with words such as *see, expect,* and *anticipate*. The text around these words should describe actions that relate to the feelings of people in the organization. The combination of future action verbs and present feelings generates energy around the vision statement that motivates associates.

Some argue that mission should come before vision; others reverse the order. I'm not sure that it really matters where you start. What does matter, however, is that you express your vision by word pictures that show people taking actions that connect their feelings with the future of the organization.

The ideal vision statement includes movement. That is, the vision statement is not like a photograph but more like an action video. The behavior-based vision has energy—people are doing things. The approach is more dynamic than static.

> *Static vision:* We will be the world's leading provider of surgical products through building a multinational sales and distribution effort.

> *Dynamic vision:* We see sales consultants demonstrating new surgical procedures to groups of physicians in Europe, China, Latin America, and the Middle East.

Notice that the static vision sounds good and communicates important information, but the dynamic vision makes it easier to visualize a salesperson calling on customers in a foreign land. By placing movement into the vision, associates are better able to see themselves carrying out its meaning.

A vision statement can reflect a goal for developing and maintaining core competencies and capabilities. This goal can then influence recruiting, selection, appraisal, coaching, and training strategies. For example, a core competency in manufacturing protein-based computer storage might be energized by presenting the vision of a manufacturing facility in which proteins coded like DNA are grown in a high-tech greenhouse. This type of wording can contribute to the excitement of a college recruiter talking about career opportunities with graduates.

A Behavior-Based Mission Statement

A traditional mission statement explains why the organization exists in terms of its overall purpose, the nature of its business, and the principles that it follows when doing business (Morrisey, 1996). It may also indicate the industry in which the organization operates and refer to values such as "human rights" or "democratic principles."

A behavior-based mission statement describes purpose and priorities in a way that suggests the direction for most of the people in the organization to take. It was made very clear to me when I was conducting a management training class for a police department. When I asked the class what their mission was, they responded in unison, "to protect, to serve, to enforce." Their mission was well rehearsed and clearly understood.

Action verbs in a mission statement describe what people are to do. Notice that this is not a highly specific, molecular description of actions to take. More general language is fine here. Remember that we are describing a broad purpose of an organization, not a specific job task. Exhibit 4.2 gives examples of verbs to use in mission statements.

A mission statement is like a compass. It identifies a purpose or reason for acting. It provides a sense of identity and direction, thus unifying individuals and establishing a basis for future actions. Potentially, a mission statement gives nobility to an objective by referring to principles and beliefs that go beyond the wants of any one person.

A mission statement is both exclusive and inclusive. By stating that the organization operates in a certain type of industry or does a certain type of work, it sets the stage for its associates to say, "We don't do that." For example, a belief about protecting the environment may exclude certain types of operating practices or product decisions. But mission clarity may suggest potential customers, international inclusion, or new applications of its technology.

Exhibit 4.2. Some Verbs to Use in a Behavior-Based Mission Statement.

To respond . . .	To qualify . . .
To explain . . .	To represent . . .
To support . . .	To train . . .
To pursue . . .	To inquire . . .
To resist . . .	To resolve . . .
To identify . . .	To negotiate . . .

The Trail Riders' Mission

I was on horseback with my wife and several other riders, moving at a brisk pace down an old road in the backwoods of Tennessee. We were competing against another group of riders in reaching Miller's Pond first. The winning group would have cold beer that afternoon and bragging rights all summer.

We knew the destination. There was a beautiful meadow with the pond to one side. It was always cool there. It was our vision to see the others ride up to us as we lounged beside the pond. This motivated us to take the old logging trail. It went through difficult terrain but in a direct route. The other team did not have the same capabilities as we, so they chose a trail that was easier but longer.

In places, the road sank deep into the terrain. The ridge on our left was a wall of earth that helped keep us going in the right direction. This ridge symbolized a mission, showing us where to go.

On the other side of the road was a second ridge, which also provided a boundary. It represented our values, guiding us along the way. We would not endanger the riders, abuse the horses, or spoil the environment as we rode along.

The ridges on each side of the road provided no absolute guarantee that we would stay on the right path. Human nature prevailed at one point where the ridge on the left was about ten feet higher than the trail. We indulged ourselves by having fun riding our horses up the incline. Although we enjoyed getting off the road for a few minutes, we returned to the trail and moved toward our vision.

Our group won. We shared a capability of being able to ride a difficult trail harder and faster than the other team. We had stronger skills than they; however, we couldn't say that our skills were unique compared with those of all other riders.

At the pond we rewarded ourselves with a cool drink and a rest in the shade. When the others arrived we jeered them without mercy. Then we enjoyed a victory ride back to the barn. It was a very profitable experience.

There should be a reciprocal relationship between a mission statement and core competencies. Each should influence the other. The resultant clarification of core competencies and mission may then lead the organization to work in new industries, thus leading to divestiture, merger, or acquisition.

> **"If you create a winning parade, sooner or later everybody else starts to follow along."**
> —Fred Smith, founder and CEO of Federal Express

Common sense argues that not all your associates agree with all the principles, understand the purpose, or care about the position of the organization. If the percentage of these associates is too great, your mission statement loses credibility and impact. If there is a critical mass in agreement with the basic thrust of your mission statement, however, the organization has the opportunity to guide the actions of disbelievers. This suggests that your mission statement needs to advance the understanding of associates but not be so far ahead that it builds cynicism. This also means that your mission statement is a tool for change. It can state principles, purpose, and position that advance understanding and acceptance.

A Behavior-Based Values Statement

A values statement describes the shared beliefs and norms that characterize the organization. It describes the standards to be used in guiding and evaluating the way people act. Often the shared values can be traced to the business philosophy held by the founders and opinion leaders. An organization's culture is a reflection of these shared values, along with the rituals, traditions, and heroes that are part of its history.

Shared values represent one of the important components of an organization's culture. Shared values penetrate the organization and go beyond slogans, making it clear what people in the organization believe are the important aspects of their work. Shared values are made tangible in a behavior-based values statement that describes what people are doing when you see the value being carried out. It converts abstract trait words such as *integrity, discipline,* or *honesty* into a description of what people do in an organization when they show the quality. For example, a value for diversity (Exhibit 4.3) can be expressed as a performance skill, followed by more specific behavioral anchors. As you look at this example keep in mind that the behavioral language is not molecular. It is stated in the most general way that will allow for reliable rating of the extent to which a person is exhibiting the value.

Although values can be defined in behavioral language, they gain their real meaning from the experiences of people in the organization. For example, in the early 1970s, I worked as a consultant for several law enforcement organizations. There were tremendous cultural differences among the organizations. The less progressive cultures had no women in patrol and only a handful of racial minorities in the command structure. Officers who were taking college classes earned the nickname of "schoolboys." The more progressive cultures encouraged education and had women and racial minorities in all jobs of the organization. There was a tremendous difference in the "feel" of the different cultures.

Edgar Schein gives a good example of how culture molds behavior in his article "Deep Culture" (Schein, 1986). He explains that it took him several months to really understand the bad manners of the executives in a high-tech firm. Over time, he discovered their assumption: Testing new ideas requires conflict. Because no one could claim to know the right answers to questions about rapid technical change, they assumed that the most effective way to get the answers was to take opposite positions on an idea and fight it out. This assumption was reflected in effective, but impolite, behavior.

One challenge in generating a values statement involves going beyond feelings about the work situation. The statement must use behavioral language to describe what people will do when they are

Exhibit 4.3. A Value for Respecting Diversity in Behavior-Based Language.

Respecting diversity: Able to adapt behavior to others' styles; interacts with people who have different values, cultures, or backgrounds; services difficult people by committing to personal responsibility for solutions; optimizes the benefits of having a diverse workforce.

Level	Behavior Description
	Does things like
5	• Initiates conversation with others who are different, even when the situation may offer barriers to communication. • Explains to others how a diverse workforce benefits the organization. • Uses respectful language during disagreement or conflict with different people. • Initiates changes that enhance the acceptance of different groups. • Shows a leadership role in diversity training. Serves as an intermediary in conflict resolution between different people. • Includes and interacts with people who are different.
4	In between
3	• Talks with others who are different, when the opportunity arises. • Listens to the ways that a diverse workforce benefits the organization. • Withdraws from conversation during disagreement or conflict with different people. • Accepts changes that enhance the acceptance of different groups. • Supports the ideas explored in diversity training. Avoids conflict with different groups. • Tolerates people who are different.
2	In between
1	• Avoids talking with others who are different. • Openly disagrees with the idea that a diverse workforce benefits the organization. • Uses profanity, blame, or stereotypes during disagreement or conflict with different people. • Rejects changes that enhance the acceptance of different groups. • Speaks against the ideas explored in diversity training. • Initiates conflict with different groups. • Rejects people who are different.

using the value. Supporting and expanding the value through the HR systems of the organization then becomes easier.

Another benefit of developing a behavior-based statement of shared values is that it helps you identify the aspects of corporate culture that work for or against performance and productive change. By making shared values behavioral, you can question or take full advantage of the culture. If you can't make values behavioral, it is much more difficult to determine which values are dysfunctional or underused.

Linking Identity to HR Applications

When an identity statement is written in behavioral language, there is an opportunity to align it with the organizational level of the competency scope. Recall that these are *core competencies and capabilities* and *core values and priorities*.

Core competencies and capabilities are tied to an organization's identity and have a reciprocal relationship with vision, mission, and values. For example, a core competency can change an organization's mission. An HR company can decide to forgo the training business and move into the consulting business because of its core competencies—or vice versa. A value or priority also can influence an organization's mission. For example, a value for health and fitness might influence a stock fund to abandon the tobacco industry and forego profitable investments.

A core competency or capability suggests technical skills and knowledge that are important for an individual to develop. For example, an accounting firm might have an electronic, high-speed audit process like the following for use in casinos:

Continuous high-speed audit: Able to devise video and computer-based monitoring systems that audit cash transfer and other transactions on a minute-by-minute basis; develops specialized accounting ratios and procedures to alert security and management of financial discrepancies; applies financial tests to tax, management information, and consulting needs of the organization for action within twenty-four hours.

In addition to a reciprocal relationship between identity and organizational characteristics, it is logical to expect organizational characteristics to influence HR systems. For example, a value such as respecting diversity would influence how the organization recruits and selects associates. In turn, you might develop a structured interview that contains a performance skill on respecting diversity, followed by related questions. You could also add other performance skills to the interview based on your organization's core values to determine the candidate's "fit" for the organization. However, HR systems need to reflect both the identity of the organization and the job requirements for specific jobs in it. It is not enough to determine whether a job candidate is a culture fit. The candidate must also have the skills needed to do a specific job.

The structural alignment of HR systems to the identity of the organization can take many forms. For example, in a selection interview, you may need to assess a candidate's technical and job skills in relation to core competencies. You should also assess the performance skills important for being able to do a specific job, as well as support the core values of the organization. Later, a performance appraisal will measure the same performance predicted by the selection interview for that job.

Coaching should relate to the performance of important job tasks and support the organization's core values. A training class should be built around instructional objectives that represent what needs to be learned to maintain core competencies and capabilities, as well as address the learning requirements for specific jobs. Everything should fit together.

Many HR systems are tactical. They respond to specific needs and governmental regulations. They become more strategic, however, when connected with the organization's identity through behavioral language. When this is done, you can say that your orga-

> The content linkage strategy is a simple way to create a line of sight between an individual and where the organization is going. Using the words in an identity statement in HR forms and procedures gives the person an experience of how the system relates to his or her needs. Once alignment is achieved, a person says, "I belong here."

nization has a strategic HR system that reinforces its identity in day-to-day decisions about people. Development of these systems requires broad participation (Exhibit 4.4) throughout the organization to refine organizational identity and to support alignment.

A relatively simple way to develop structural alignment involves the application of the procedures used to provide evidence for the content validity of an interview or test. Remember that content validation shows that the items in a test closely match the domain of information to be measured by the test. For example, a test in basic mathematics would contain questions on addition, subtraction, multiplication, and division.

When the content of an identity statement is reflected in the content of HR forms and processes, we have *content linkage*. In its simplest form, content linkage means that the very same words used in an identity statement are also found in the behavior-based competencies used with selection, appraisal, coaching, and training. For example, the following words were used in an identity statement: "provide *one-day* international service." The following words were incorporated into a performance skill involving coping: "respond to demanding customers while competing the service cycle in *one day*." Notice that the phrase "one day" is included in both the identity and the competency.

Exhibit 4.5 is an example of connecting identity to the specifics of HR systems.

At this point I need to do a little public relations for the content linkage strategy. Frankly, I know that it is easy for you to be

Exhibit 4.4. Opportunities for Participation.

Identity	Create mixed teams of executives, managers, and individual contributors for developing an identity statement.
Interviews	Involve job experts in creating structured interviews.
Performance	Come to an agreement on performance expectations.
Coaching	Jointly convert task statements into goal statements.
Training	Use intact work teams and course designers to create instructional objectives.

thinking something like the following: "You are telling me that it is good to lift the words from our corporate identity and put them into our HR systems. I'm not sure that I want to try to sell this to my organization. It doesn't sound very exciting."

Probably the best way to tackle this concern is to explore your vision of what a competency project really means. If your vision is cramped, you are seeing yourself attempting to explain these ideas to a resistant group of coworkers who are themselves concerned about wasting money and making mistakes. On the other hand, an open vision means that you can see yourself meeting with any group in your organization and asking questions about such things as the direction of the organization, their work team, and their careers. Remember the cart-before-the-horse analogy—put the horse up front so it can pull the cart. Here the horse is the individual's pain, sense of ambiguity, and concern about what to do on the job. Once you open up these issues, content linkage is the cart that shows people how to begin to redesign their work lives.

This reminds me of a time in my career when I was very frustrated when making a presentation to people who didn't want to hear about research, needed change, or problems. A fellow consultant who was far wiser than I coached me on how to use presentation time to help my audience think of a problem they experienced and then relate my message to their problem. When his advice is

Exhibit 4.5. Connect Identity to HR Applications.

Here is an example of moving from a virtue-based identity into a behavior-based statement and then using content linkage to align a performance skill, interview question, and rating anchors.

Virtue-based identity phrase:	We are persistent, innovative *problem solvers*.
Behavior-based identity phrase:	We *spend enough time* to thoroughly *define problems* and describe the steps needed to *solve* them.
Inclusion in a performance skill:	*Problem* solving: Able to write a problem *definition* by describing the facts that caused the *problem* to be noticed; gathers potential solutions from people close to the *problem*; identifies the *steps* needed in implementing a *solution*.
Interview question for a specific job:	Describe a time when you used your engineering skills to help you identify the *steps* to take in *defining* a work *problem* and generating a *solution*.
Rating anchors for scoring the answer:	High: *Spent enough time to objectively define the problem* in writing and listed the *steps to solve* it. Described how personal feelings were managed while *solving* the *problem*.
	Average: Took *some time to define* the *problem* and developed a general plan for *solving* it; controlled personal feelings while *solving* the *problem*.
	Low: Did not take *enough time* to *define* the *problem* or develop a plan for *solving* it; reacted to the *problem* in a way that hindered its *solution*.

applied to your possible concerns about the content linkage strategy, it makes sense to think of your building a shared vision for how this idea relates to the needs of your organization. Content linkage is not more work to do. It is one way to deal with the ambiguity people feel on their jobs.

Summary and Preview

The identity of an organization includes its core competencies, capabilities, core values, and priorities. When identity is expressed in behavioral language, it is more likely to be understood and applied by individuals in the organization.

The personal alignment of associates with the overall organization comes from participation. Structural alignment occurs when the systems and procedures of the organization clearly reflect its identity. A practical way to encourage participation is to involve associates in linking the content of an identity statement to the technical and performance skills described in HR procedures and forms. The next section will show how this can be done, beginning with the involvement of job experts in developing a job-related, structured interview that also reflects the identity of the organization.

Part II

Linking Competencies to Human Resource Systems

This section offers a way to link interviews, appraisals, coaching, and training to the identity of an organization. It emphasizes a systematic, job-related approach to support the effectiveness and defensibility of an HR system.

The applications model will guide our thinking in this section. Essentially, it says that (1) a structured process with clear procedures is preferable to an intuitive process, and (2) a job-related, behavioral approach is more practical than a whole-person, attribute-based approach. The use of the behavioral approach also sets the stage for the effective linkage of human resource systems to an organization's identity.

As shown in Figure P2.1, the applications model suggests that there are four organizational approaches that influence the types of human resource systems that are put into place. Each of these approaches differs in the extent to which it is driven by perception, experience, attributes, or behavior.

The four approaches can be summarized as follows:

Perception-driven The perception-driven organization is more intuitive and feeling oriented. The HR system in this organization places less emphasis on being specific, gathering information, and measuring. Its HR efforts will rely on gut-feel interviews, likability appraisal, motivational coaching, and smile training. There is a deemphasis on structured, job-related, human resource systems.

Figure P2.1. The Applications Model.

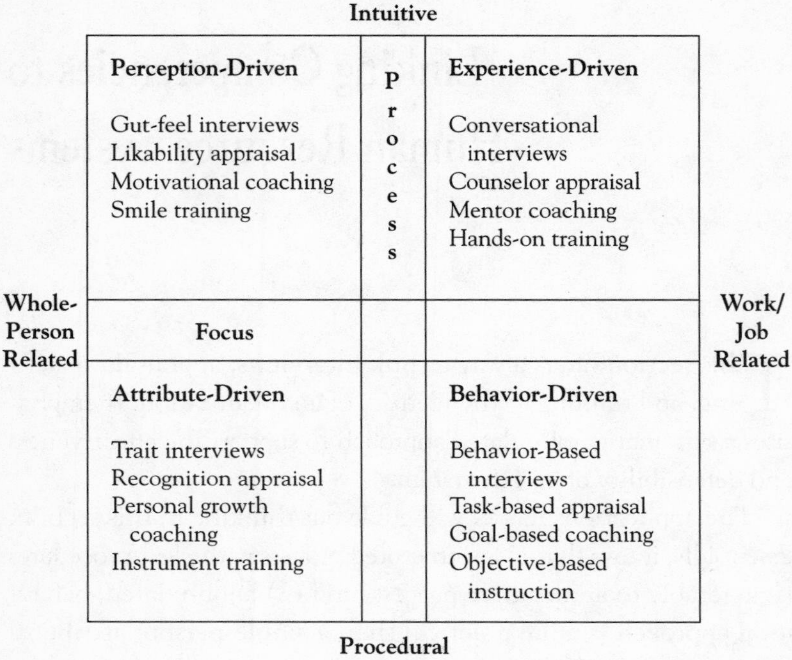

Intuitive

Perception-Driven Gut-feel interviews Likability appraisal Motivational coaching Smile training	P r o c e s s	**Experience-Driven** Conversational interviews Counselor appraisal Mentor coaching Hands-on training
Focus		

Attribute-Driven
 	
Trait interviews
Recognition appraisal
Personal growth
  coaching
Instrument training
		Behavior-Driven
		
		Behavior-Based
		  interviews
		Task-based appraisal
		Goal-based coaching
		Objective-based
		  instruction

Whole-Person Related (left)   Work/Job Related (right)

Procedural

Consequently, this HR approach is less likely to generate defensible, reliable, and valid measures of a person's skills.

Experience-driven The experience-driven organization uses work experience in an intuitive way. The experience of individual managers is the cornerstone for conversational interviews, counselor appraisal, mentor coaching, and hands-on training. This approach can be effective with capable managers. However, this organization is less likely to receive the benefits of well-designed work systems and loses wisdom when capable people leave.

Attribute-driven An organization that emphasizes attributes uses trait words to describe people. All of a person's characteristics are considered, regardless of the extent to which they are used in a current work assignment. HR systems are based on trait-driven interviews, recognition appraisal, personal growth coaching, and instrument training. The effective use of this approach requires more training in the behavioral sciences than is usually afforded to managers. Also, the use of the traits may increase stereotyping, weaken defensibility, and complicate the linkage of human resource functions.

Behavior-driven When an organization adopts the behavior-driven strategy, it emphasizes observation, description, and cautious inferences about people. The combined emphasis on procedures and the work to be done improves the reliability and validity of the application. This approach involves behavior-based interviews, task-based appraisal, goal-based coaching, and objective-based instruction. Behavioral language is used to reinforce the goals of the organization and improve measurement.

The linkage of HR applications is easier when the organization consistently uses a behavioral approach. Once behavioral language is used in one part of an HR system, it can be expanded to other applications.

In Chapter Five you will see how the applications model can distinguish between different approaches to selection interviews. The model then will guide our discussion of appraisal (Chapter Six), coaching (Chapter Seven), and training (Chapter Eight). Each chapter explains how to use the behavioral approach to reflect an organization's identity and specific job requirements.

Behavior-Based Interviewing

The best predictor of future behavior is past behavior.
William Owens (1976)

I once served as part of an interview team, providing my assessment of job candidates along with a group of interviewers from an organization that had just rolled out the Behavioral Interviewing® Seminar. During one debriefing, a bright but as yet untrained interviewer said that the candidate was "a jerk" and that interviewing him was a "waste of time." Another interviewer (who had obviously listened well in class) asked, "What did you see or hear that makes you say this person is a jerk?"

As you can imagine, the discussion moved toward using behavioral language. Ultimately, the "jerk" candidate was described in terms of his actions:

- He interrupted the interviewer at least seven times.

- He used sexist language.

- He pointed his finger at an interviewer and spoke loudly.

- He made critical comments about his last three employers.

These interviewers took one person's gut feeling and converted it into a description of what the candidate did that caused a negative reaction. In the process of making this transition from a trait to a behavior, everyone learned how to be very specific in describing the actions that lead up to the inference.

You might think that the gut-feeling approach and the Behavioral Interviewing® system would probably have produced the same results. This candidate was an obvious mismatch for the job, whether the interviewer simply felt that the candidate was a jerk or whether the interviewer listed inappropriate behaviors. It is important to remember, however, that you need the behavioral approach to help you make effective decisions when the mismatch is not as obvious.

One of the most difficult challenges faced by a new interviewer is to go beyond a gut feeling and gather behavioral information about a candidate's job-related skills. Many interviewers assume that they are intuitively skilled at "figuring people out." The most solid approach, however, is to use information on past behavior to guide a selection decision.

A second challenge faced by today's interviewer is to avoid the temptation to assess *only* a candidate's fit to the organization. Remember that the defense of a selection procedure is based on the extent to which it is job related. An interview that is based only on a candidate's fit to an organization will not measure the skills needed to do the job itself. For example, a person may share the values of a charitable organization but not be able to get donations.

The behavior-based interviewing strategy can assess the extent to which a person is both a fit for the organization and able to do a particular job. As you will see, the behavioral approach can use performance skills that reflect the organization's identity, or *work context*, and job requirements, or *job content*. This enables an interviewer to ask questions about the skills that are needed to do a job well in a particular organization.

Approaches to Interviewing

The applications model described in the introduction to Part Two distinguishes between the different approaches used by interviewers. The horizontal scale of the model shows the kinds of information the interviewer tries to get from the candidate, ranging from *whole person–oriented* on the left of the Figure to work to *job related* on the right. The vertical scale, which shows how the interviewer gathers and manages information, ranges from *intuitive* to *procedural*. When combined, the two scales suggest four distinct approaches to interviewing.

Gut-Feel Interviews

This person-oriented, intuitive approach uses the interviewer's "gut feel" as the standard for assessing the candidate. The interviewer does not use a structured interview with job-related questions. Instead, questions are spontaneously asked in light of the interviewer's reactions to the candidate. In this type of interview, subjective criteria are used to interpret the answers, and general impressions serve as the basis for selection. A major disadvantage of this approach is that the selection decision may reflect the interviewer's personal theories and beliefs about people. This means that decisions can be influenced by trivial things such as appearance or by illegal biases based on gender, race, color, religion, national origin, age, or disabilities.

Conversational Interviews

This approach involves an unstructured interview with a focus on the candidate's job experience and job skills. It resembles a conversation between two equals. Questions about work experiences arise in the flow of conversation, not from a prepared list. The conversation often branches naturally from one topic to another, based on the candidate's responses and the interviewer's knowledge of the job. This style relaxes the candidate, allowing him to reveal additional details about qualifications and character. A disadvantage of this approach is that the conversational interviewer must be a very capable person who knows the job very well. Also, failure to use a structured interview weakens the defensibility of the selection process.

Trait Interviews

A trait interview uses a structured approach that is oriented to the total person. It measures key personality traits such as conscientiousness, likability, adjustment, creativity, and drive. In a well-designed trait interview, the interviewer reads questions from a structured interview form. These questions relate more to the personal characteristics of the total person than to specific work-related skills. With a structured approach, sometimes enhanced by personality testing, a trait interview can be effective in assessing crucial personality traits needed for a specific job. But a good trait interviewer needs more training than a manager typically gets. An untrained person can easily stereotype a candidate with trait words.

Behavior-Based Interviews

A behavior-based interview is structured, like the trait interview, and job focused, like the conversational style. However, the structured interview form asks singular, open-ended questions about past events in the candidate's work experiences, thus soliciting evidence for job-related skills from the candidate's background. The interviewer takes descriptive notes during the interview and rates the candidate's skills for doing the job by comparing examples of past performance to skill definitions. The interviewer then bases a selection decision on the overall match of skills to job requirements.

There are many reasons for using the behavior-based interviewing strategy. First, there is evidence that the technique is both reliable and valid (Campion, Campion, and Hudson, 1994; Campion,

Palmer, and Campion, 1997; Green, Alter, and Carr, 1993; Janz, 1982; McDaniel, Whetzel, Schmidt, and Maurer, 1994; Motowidlo and others, 1992; Orpen, 1985; Pulakos and Schmitt, 1995; Weisner and Cronshaw, 1988). The structure and job-related aspects of these interviews provide good measurement, prediction, and defensibility. A survey conducted by the American Compensation Association showed that very few legal challenges were associated with the competency-based interviewing technique used with the behavior-based approach (1996). A review of 130 federal court cases showed that many of the components in the behavior-based strategy are related to favorable verdicts for defendants (Gollub and others, 1997).

A second reason for using the behavior-based approach is that the behavioral language provides the basis for linking organizational identity to the interviewing system. As discussed in Chapter Four, this is accomplished by using the same words and phrases in the behavior-based identity statement and in the structured interview.

The best way to develop an interviewing system that links HR to identity is to use a *top-down and bottoms-up approach*. Input from the organization's identity tends to come from the top of the organization, whereas the job requirements primarily come from the level in the organization at which the job is done. A structured interview can be developed from input from both directions (Figure 5.1).

Many organizations build their interviewing systems entirely around core values. There is a big problem with this approach, though it's not very obvious. Developing an interviewing system from identity down to HR systems only includes the *context* of jobs. You must build selection tools around the *content* of specific jobs as well. Then it's OK to include important aspects of the work context, such as culture and values, into the selection interview.

According to the Civil Rights Act of 1991, an employer's defense against discrimination is based on the requirement that the process be "job related and consistent with business necessity." Similarly, the

Figure 5.1. A Structured Interview Can Combine the Work Context and the Job Content.

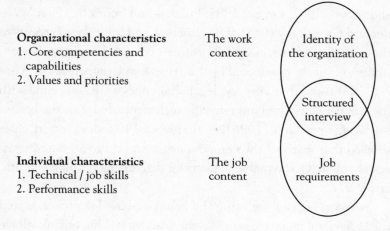

Organizational characteristics
1. Core competencies and capabilities
2. Values and priorities

The work context

Identity of the organization

Structured interview

Individual characteristics
1. Technical / job skills
2. Performance skills

The job content

Job requirements

Americans with Disabilities Act (1991) indicates that you need to be prepared to modify essential job functions as part of the process of accommodating the needs of a disabled person. These functions relate primarily to the important tasks performed in a specific job and secondarily to the organization's core values. This reflects how traditional *job analysis* is being expanded to *work analysis*, which will also account for work flow, teams, and job change (Sanchez, 1994).

A Behavior-Based Interviewing System

There are many benefits to using a systematic approach to interviewing. A systematic approach

- Results in the development of job-related, structured interviews for a variety of positions in the organization

- Shows interviewers how to gather job-related information, make decisions based on skills for the job, and avoid subjective, gut-feel decisions

- Helps interviewers avoid asking the same questions of each candidate

- Enables interviewers to speak the same language when comparing their assessments of candidates

- Makes it possible to link interviewing to other HR systems, such as appraisal

- Suggests information to be covered in interview training

A behavior-based interview is a structured interview that contains singular, open-ended questions about past events that can provide evidence regarding a job candidate's skills. It is based on an analysis of the job and is administered in a systematic way. Once the interview is complete, ratings are made by comparing information about the candidate's past behavior to job-related skill definitions. This encourages the use of objective information about a candidate's skills in making a selection decision. This approach has five steps (Figure 5.2), which are repeated if there is a significant change in the job under analysis.

Figure 5.2. The Steps of Behavior-Based Interviewing.

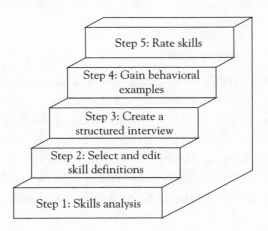

Step 1: Skills Analysis

A skills analysis is a systematic process of identifying the technical/job skills and performance skills important for doing a job well. It is a type of job analysis that addresses both the job content and the work context, including core competencies, capabilities, values, and priorities. There are several important elements of a skills analysis.

Identify Job Experts

A job expert, sometimes called a subject-matter expert, possesses in-depth knowledge of how to perform a job in the work context of the organization. This knowledge comes from experiences such as actually doing the job, supervising people who do the job, receiving special training, or observing the job being done.

Job experts are able to give an accurate description of what needs to be done to do the job well. This approach is very different from the in-depth study of high performers. Admittedly, high performers do some things that are very important for job success. However, we have all seen high performers who do some things wrong. There are also some low performers who do some things well. Job experts can identify what needs to be done in the job based on their collective experiences and observations of how others do the job.

Assemble Job Information

A skills-analysis coordinator collects existing information on the job and organization, documents the qualifications of job experts, and directs the job experts on the steps of the work analysis (see Exhibit 5.1). Completion of this step is very important if you want your work to have a high level of defensibility.

Notice that the list of information to be assembled includes an organizational identity statement and task statements from a job

Exhibit 5.1. Job Information to Consider When Preparing for a Skills Analysis.

- An organizational identity statement
- A values statement
- A culture statement
- A job description
- Previous job studies
- Validation studies
- Competency studies
- Task statements from a job analysis
- Job analysis results
- Generic competency models
- Statements of minimum job qualifications for the position
- A job summary from the *Dictionary of Occupational Titles*
- Projected job duties for a new position
- A strategic business plan
- Names of previous incumbents
- A statement of human resource policy and procedures

---

analysis. This enables the job experts to include information systematically on the work context and the job content in the skills analysis.

Identify Important Work Activities

A questionnaire approach to skills analysis is cost effective with large-scale projects. Jobholders meet in small groups and rate a standard list of statements that describe the important things to do on a job. The most frequently rated activities are then combined into skill definitions.

This approach is based on the development of a list of activity statements that reasonably reflect the "footprint" of work done in the organization. The statements are then linked to performance skills and questions for easy selection by interviewers. Using the questionnaire approach means rating the importance of the activity for the job, referring to the question that is linked to it, and then editing the question if necessary.

Here is an example of an activity statement that you would rate in terms of its importance for doing a job.

Cope with strict deadlines or time demands.

Remember that this activity statement would have already been linked to a performance skill and interview question. For example, the performance skill would be

Coping: Able to request and provide relevant information while responding to interpersonal conflict, personal rejection, hostility, or time demands; avoids outbursts of temper and destructive behavior; does not express negative feelings to customers.

And the interview question would be

Give me an example of a time when you had to cope with strict deadlines and time demands.

Because all of the activities are linked to questions, you would be able to develop a job-related, structured interview quickly.

Specify Essential Job Functions

The identification of essential job functions is important if you need to have an HR system that effectively reflects the requirements of the Americans with Disabilities Act. Knowledge of essential job functions helps you accommodate the special needs of a disabled worker. The regulations of the Equal Employment Opportunity Commission define essential job functions as follows: "The term 'essential functions' means the fundamental job duties of the employment position the individual with a disability holds or desires. The term 'essential functions' does not include the marginal functions of the position" (Equal Employment Opportunity Commission, 1992).

An essential job function directly relates to the central purpose of the job. Most jobs have a limited number of essential job functions—six to twelve is normal. During a skills analysis, you can determine whether a job function is essential by asking the job experts to rate each activity or task as to importance, frequency, duration, and consequences of an error. This in turn will provide justification for asking questions of a candidate with a disability.

Skills Analysis Versus Individual Analysis

"We need people with a killer instinct who can sell bonds right now," one client demanded a few years ago. "I want you to develop a selection system that will get me people just like Jack. He is our best performer, and the customers worship the ground he walks on. If you can make this happen, I will make you rich."

Needless to say, this got my attention. I was intrigued as well by the challenge of developing a system that I could validate with a dollar criterion. If the system worked, it should generate more money. Naturally, my first question was, "When can I talk to Jack?"

I soon discovered that star-performer Jack was a gregarious, old-style "bond daddy." He exhibited charm and ruthlessness at the same time. His sales strategy involved heavy entertainment and development of customer rapport, techniques that made people look forward to seeing him. He was technically honest in everything that he did, but it would be stretching the truth to say that he gave customers good deals.

Jack was not the only top performer. Admittedly, for this company at this particular time, he was number one. However, there were many other roads to sales success. There were probably lots of tactics that even Jack was not using that could make another person very successful. For example, one of the company's most successful new associates was technical, introverted, and uncomfortable in social situations. He was very different from Jack but nevertheless was skilled in doing the work.

Consequently, we developed a selection system based on the important things that anyone should do to be successful in this job. To gaze only at one top performer, or even a small group of them, means that you aren't looking at the remaining universe of important actions that lead to success.

My conclusion is that the best way to understand the predictors of job success begins with a skills analysis, not an individual analysis. Begin your skills analysis with the selection of job experts. They may be top performers, but the focus is on describing what needs to be done on the job rather than explaining what the top performers are like as individuals. With this information, the job experts can systematically explore all of the factors that lead to job success.

If a candidate cannot adequately respond to a question based on an essential job function, a discussion of reasonable accommodations should be carried out. According to the Americans with Disabilities Act, it is important to accommodate a disability by redesigning the job or reassigning essential job tasks. To make these accommodations, it is desirable to have identified the essential job tasks and the questions developed around them before the interview.

Step 2: Select and Edit Skill Definitions

Once you have completed the skills analysis, the next step is to develop skill definitions for the technical/job skills and performance skills important for doing the job. There are two ways to do this.

In the first approach, the job experts can develop the skill definitions from scratch. The activities and tasks that are important in doing the job well are organized into similar groups. The skill definitions are then built around the groupings and all of the other information about the job and the organization.

The second approach is much quicker and yields comparable results. Here the job experts use a questionnaire to generate a job profile. They then select and customize generic skill definitions. These definitions are edited so that they contain phrasing from the identity statement as well as specific job requirements.

Exhibit 5.2 shows how you can tailor a performance skill to reflect your own organization's values and job requirements. Notice that the wording in the edited skill definition contains many phrases from the generic definition. But it also contains phrases from the organization's mission statement and job tasks, thus adapting the generic skill definition to both the work context and the job content.

There are many advantages to having job experts edit prewritten performance skills. You are able to suggest the language to be edited, and editing a prewritten performance skill is much easier than developing one from the ground up. A disadvantage to this approach is that the more a performance skill is edited, the less likely it is to benefit from any research used in developing the generic version.

Step 3: Create a Structured Interview

When I speak of a structured interview, I am referring to a list of preplanned questions from which an interviewer may choose during the interview. Sometimes called a *patterned interview,* this approach enables the interviewer to select the best questions to ask the candidate during the interview itself.

A highly structured interview requires the interviewer to ask the same questions in the same order for each candidate. Each answer is scored by comparing it to scoring guides that reflect the degree to which the answer is poor, good, or superior. Sometimes this interview is described as a *linear interview.* Resources A and B give examples of a structured interview and a highly structured interview.

There is substantial evidence that structure is important for determining interview reliability (Campion, Palmer, and Campion,

Exhibit 5.2. How to Link a Mission Statement and a Job's Requirements to a Behavior-Based Interview.

Here is a mission statement:

> Our mission is to provide timely accounting services worldwide through building service relationships, continuously improving the technology for meeting customer needs, and accommodating cultural differences, for manufacturers of consumer electronics.

Here is a generic, behavior-based performance skill taken from the list of competencies in Chapter One:

> Team participation: Works cooperatively with others and contributes to the group with ideas, suggestions, and effort; communicates acceptance or rejection of team commitments; does not talk about team members in a negative manner in their absence; is willing to confront performance problems of the team.

A job in market development for this organization uses a team sales approach. Two of the important tasks to be done in this job are

1. Cooperate with members of the sales team in order to provide a timely response to customer requests.
2. Speak out in team meetings on ways to improve team performance in order to meet the needs of culturally different customers.

The generic version of team participation is edited to reflect parts of the mission statement and tasks required of persons on the market development team. Notice that the wording reflects the inclusion of words and phrases in both the mission statement and job tasks.

> Teamwork: Able to build a *service relationship* with internal/external customers by giving a *timely response to requests* and *accommodating cultural differences*; contributes to *continuous improvement* with ideas, suggestions, and effort; avoids talking about team members negatively in their absence; *describes possible performance improvements to better meet customer needs*.

Here are two interview questions developed from the edited performance skill:

1. Describe a time when you were able to be cooperative with a difficult coworker to give *a timely response to a customer*.
2. Give me an example of a time when you were able to build a *service relationship* with a customer who was *culturally different* from you.

Notice that these questions reflect the mission statement and specific job tasks for a person on the sales team.

1997). With a reliable interview, two or more interviewers will tend to agree on their ratings of the candidate. Without structure, the interview is much less effective in measuring a candidate's skills for the job.

A structured interview that is behavior based can contain questions that are related to both the work context and the job content. The work context is reflected in language that describes the core competencies, capabilities, core values, and priorities that are justifiable selection criteria. Job relatedness is reflected in the design of each question to reflect either a technical/job skill or performance skill important for the job. This means that you should develop different structured interviews for different jobs, because job requirements naturally vary from position to position.

The behavior-based approach is characterized by its use of singular, open-ended questions about past events. Here are some examples of behavior-based questions:

Give me an example of a time when you worked hard to get results.

Describe a situation in which you were particularly effective in getting organized.

Tell me about a time when you were creative at work.

These questions are organized under the performance skills important for doing the job. You can see more of these questions in the structured interview and the highly structured interview in the Resources section at the end of the book.

How much time is required for developing a structured interview that is related to both the work context and job content? My estimate is that with computerized support, three to five job experts working together need about two hours to create a structured interview. This is close to the amount of time needed for enough participation of job experts to have enough buy-in to cause people actually to use the process.

Step 4: Gain Behavioral Examples

A behavioral example is a job candidate's description of a specific time that he used a skill. If you ask a past-event question, you help the candidate think of a behavioral example. However, simply asking the question is not enough. Often the candidate responds to a past-event question by giving a self-description or a trait response, or the candidate may respond with a generality about his skills.

Typically, a job candidate breaks eye contact before providing a behavioral example, probably to concentrate while thinking. When the candidate resumes eye contact you will typically hear a behavioral example or a question for clarification.

You can identify whether the example is behavioral by noting whether it shows what the candidate did in a particular situation. Behavioral examples always contain some specific information on the situation in which the person took action. This reference includes some combination of names, dates, numbers, times, and locations.

I have found that candidates are quite able to give specific examples in response to most behavior-based questions. For example, we conducted a validation study of the Behavioral Interviewing technique with the Arizona Highway Patrol (Green, Alter, and Carr, 1993). In this study, we asked forty-six officers 12 questions each—a total of 552 questions. In these interviews, only one candidate could not answer one question. This means that the interview panel gained behavioral examples 99 percent of the time.

Behavioral examples give you events from the candidate's background to compare to job-related skill definitions. Your selection decision can be based on the extent to which the person has the skills needed for a specific job. You are not assessing the attributes of the whole person—only his or her job-related skills.

Step 5: Rate Skills

In the final step of the Behavioral Interviewing system you evaluate the interview responses through a process called *tri-*

angulation (Figure 5.3). Using this approach, you complete the following three steps:

1. Read the skill definition specifying what to measure. For example:

Coping: Able to request and provide relevant information while responding to interpersonal conflict, personal rejection, hostility, or time demands; avoids outbursts of temper and destructive behavior; does not express negative feelings to customers.

2. Read all of the notes you took in the interview. It is essential to have thorough notes, taken in a direct-quote format, to rate skills effectively.

3. Compare your interview notes to the skill definition by using the rating-scale anchors. In most cases, you can use general anchors that compare and rate the presence or absence of the skill. It is also possible to have very detailed anchors, which you use to rate each answer to the interview questions. You

Figure 5.3. Rating Skills Based on Interview Performance.

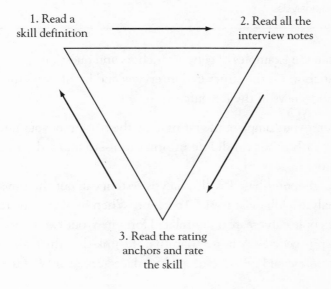

1. Read a skill definition

2. Read all the interview notes

3. Read the rating anchors and rate the skill

A Practical Example

I once contributed to a participative and time-efficient competency-based skills analysis with a large trucking company. We had the challenge of developing selection interviews and performance-rating forms for two new and very important positions. The skills analysis involved two teams of six job experts each. Each job expert was aware of the expectations associated with doing the new jobs.

The teams spent one day following the skills analysis procedures to develop a structured interview and a performance-rating form for each job. They cross-checked each other's work, participating heavily and cutting lunch short to get the work done. This was a very thorough approach with a large number of job experts participating in the skills analysis. Consequently, about fourteen person–work days were required to develop the interviews and appraisal forms for two jobs.

I was able to speed up the work considerably on a consulting job with a heavy manufacturing company. A total of eight people spent half a day creating and cross-checking sets of interview and appraisal forms. This project went faster because the job was well established and the job experts were HR professionals who were experienced in job analysis.

can see examples of generic anchors and question-specific anchors on the structured interview and highly structured interviews in the Resources.

After you complete the ratings, use the pattern of your ratings—along with other candidate information—to make the selection decision.

A computer-based skills-analysis system can cut the time spent to analyze a job by at least 50 percent. When in place, one team of four people can create a job-related form in about two hours. If the work proceeded any faster than that, I think that the time for participation would suffer, resulting in reduced acceptance of the work.

The costs of developing structured interviews are small when you consider the cost of making mistakes in hiring. Developing structured interviews also provides a meaningful way to build participation. The skills analysis gives many people at all levels of the organization the opportunity to speak their minds about the organization's purpose and what should be done in specific jobs to achieve that purpose.

The steps involved in developing and using behavior-based interviews will be reapplied, with some editing, to appraisal, coaching, and training. A more efficient development process will result, because much of the work in developing a structured interview will contribute to development and linkage of other applications. As you see this use of the model, please understand that the last step is followed by practical use and an eventual return to the earlier stages of the model for revisions and updates.

Summary and Preview

The appeal of simply converting the language from your organization's identity statement into a structured interview for use with all candidates for all jobs is tempting. However, each job should have its own structured interview that reflects both the job *content*, or organizational identity, and job *context*, or job tasks.

The next chapter will show how skill definitions can be used to link a structured interview and an appraisal form to an organization's identity. This is accomplished by using the same performance skills to organize questions on a structured interview and task statements on a performance discussion form.

6

Task-Based Appraisal

The best appraisal is self-appraisal.

Paul Green

There is a lot of negative energy around what is traditionally called performance appraisal. Consultants advise us to not do it, while attorneys say you had better do it! Capable managers think of it as a process, but many jobholders see it as an event. For some, it's the time to talk about a salary increase, but for others it is a put down. And we all know that it should improve performance, but it may actually weaken results by dividing teams.

A convention I attended several years ago allowed me to personally experience how intensely people feel about performance appraisal. One session I attended was in a room with about twenty tables covered with red-checkered tablecloths and ample supplies of cheese, crackers, and drinks. A facilitator stood at each table, prepared to explain the approach used in her organization. We were invited to visit as many tables as we wished, joining any conversation that met our individual needs.

Like everyone else, I started table hopping, looking for any discussion that would give me a new perspective. By the time I was at the fifth table, I sensed that most of the people in the room were mainly interested in collecting appraisal forms that they could copy and use. Although the facilitators planned to talk about their performance management systems, most participants were focused on collecting as many performance appraisal forms as possible. Frankly, I was turned off. So I asked a facilitator to explore with the group at her table why there was so much interest in appraisal forms over performance management systems.

"The interest in forms may seem superficial," she said. "But in my experience the practical value of a form is that it structures a performance discussion between a manager and the jobholder . . . and the form is what you look at if you go to court!"

"Yeah, but appraisal doesn't really contribute to performance improvement," a dissident voice proclaimed. "The best way to improve performance is to involve people in developing and improving work systems. That's why the quality movement and teams are so important."

Then the discussion got heated. It was as though the group was divided into armies in battle. On one side, there was a belief that a

---

A Survey on Performance Appraisal Practices

We conducted a survey of 162 individuals in corporations ranging in size from 500 to more than 50,000 employees on their appraisal practices. Our objective was to discover how and why appraisal was done.

We found that performance appraisal was seen as being useful in providing feedback to the jobholder. It also was beneficial in setting goals and communicating work expectations. These findings reminded me of the old saying, "Don't throw the baby out with the bath."

But the problems with appraisal were also underscored. The survey showed an overall dissatisfaction with performance appraisal— 57 percent said their employees were minimally pleased, dissatisfied, or very dissatisfied with their performance-appraisal system. A lot of this dissatisfaction probably stemmed from their performance appraisals not having yielded expected salary increases. In this case, performance appraisal failed its own appraisal.

one-on-one appraisal of performance was essential for things such as recognition, promotion, and compensation. The other side followed the admonition of W. Edwards Deming: "Performance appraisal . . . just stop doing it" (Mohrman, 1990; Scholtes, 1990; Walton, 1991).

The exchange got so heated that voices were raised and fingers were pointed. Both sides had legitimate points to make. On one hand, a case can be made that a one-on-one discussion of individual performance is important.

- A measure of individual performance can influence rewards, improvement, employment, goal setting, and expectations.

- Many people at work cannot practically participate in a team discussion on quality improvement.

- Documentation of individual performance is important for making employment decisions. Individuals are terminated, not teams.

- Some government agencies are required by law to conduct annual performance appraisals.

- Labor unions often insist on documentation of performance problems before a person can be disciplined or terminated.

- Many organizations will continue to use an authoritative approach to management, which is consistent with the approach used in traditional appraisal.

On the other hand, eliminating traditional performance appraisal can be justified for several reasons.

- On average, appraisal just doesn't do a good job in assessment or communications.

- It is a questionable part of any compensation system; annual or semi-annual appraisal is rarely able to measure

effectively what a person has singly done to cause
work outcomes.

- When an appraisal is linked to compensation the
  individual has an incentive not to admit mistakes.
  Linking pay to appraisal limits the opportunity for
  honest feedback.

- Appraisal reflects the top-down hierarchical organization in which individuals are told about performance
  rather than asked about improvement.

- Traditional appraisal generates individual competition
  and fear, not support and confidence.

- Documentation of performance focuses on the past,
  while continuous discussion of performance deals
  with immediate challenges.

- Performance improvement often comes from teams
  that continuously monitor their own performance;
  a one-on-one appraisal can actually hurt this process.

I don't plan to take sides on whether appraisal is good or bad.
And I don't plan to push hard on performance management as an
alternative to appraisal. But I do know that amid all of these pros
and cons on appraisal, there is a manager somewhere who needs to
do something like tell a customer service agent how to handle more
complaints per hour. He has two years of college, three hours of
training in appraisal, and modest interpersonal skills. He wants to
help his people do the job better, but he doesn't know what to say.

This manager and others like him need to be able to communicate about performance in a way that is comfortable, defensible, and
effective. He doesn't want theory, coaching sessions, or a video to
watch. He needs to know what to say tomorrow when he talks
about a sensitive issue to an associate who he feels shouldn't have
been hired in the first place. If we can deal with this type of prob-

lem, we have the foundation for moving into a more elegant, systematic approach for dealing with performance issues.

This is where a well-designed, job-related, performance discussion form can be of help. A form can help managers feel secure. A form also guides a discussion by suggesting what to talk about. And a form gives a manager and the jobholder something to look at when dealing with uncomfortable issues. A form can absorb tension.

The form can be on paper or on a computer screen—where it is doesn't matter. What is important is that the form describes exactly what the person is supposed to do on the job. Then it can guide regular performance discussions, weekly if you choose, that reinforce the organization's identity and specifically address what the person needs to do to do a job well.

Once a good form is developed, it can guide a two-way discussion of performance that will improve the likelihood that there will be good feelings and productive change. Effective participation around what needs to be done contributes to commitment and buy-in. In contrast, one-way ratings of performance on even a good form cannot be expected to have a consistently positive impact on performance.

In making these points I have elected to be flexible in the terminology that I use. I want to recognize that the traditional use of the word *appraisal* implies one-way, judgmental, and arbitrary evaluations of a person's work. *Performance management* is a more reasonable alternative, as it reflects the continuous nature of performance improvement, recognizing the importance of effective management, work systems, and team contributions. In addition, *performance communications* or *performance discussion* seems to do a good job of reflecting the more intangible parts of a relationship that influence performance. For more on all of these topics, consult Benardin and Beatty, 1984; Grote, 1996; and Latham and Wexley, 1994.

I have chosen to resolve this problem of terminology by using the phrase that seems to best fit the point I am making. Regardless of the term I use at any one time in discussion, the broad meaning is that systematic observation, reliable measurement, job-related focus, and participative discussion of performance is desirable.

Approaches to Appraisal

The applications model suggests that there are four appraisal strategies. The strategies reflect different ways to emphasize intuition or procedures in dealing with the whole person or work-related skills. As you will see, task appraisal is presented as the most likely strategy for linking a performance discussion to selection interviews and the organization's identity.

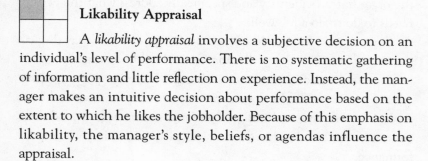

Likability Appraisal

A *likability appraisal* involves a subjective decision on an individual's level of performance. There is no systematic gathering of information and little reflection on experience. Instead, the manager makes an intuitive decision about performance based on the extent to which he likes the jobholder. Because of this emphasis on likability, the manager's style, beliefs, or agendas influence the appraisal.

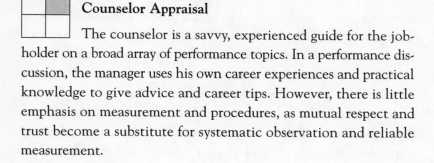

Counselor Appraisal

The counselor is a savvy, experienced guide for the jobholder on a broad array of performance topics. In a performance discussion, the manager uses his own career experiences and practical knowledge to give advice and career tips. However, there is little emphasis on measurement and procedures, as mutual respect and trust become a substitute for systematic observation and reliable measurement.

Recognition Appraisal

In this approach, the discussion moves toward recognition of a person's positive qualities and traits, a direction that is good. However, recognition is only part of the appraisal process.

Without specific actions to recognize, the discussion may only reward efforts, not outcomes. Recognition of general qualities and traits shifts the focus from job performance to individual characteristics.

Task-Based Appraisal

The manager and jobholder systematically collect descriptions of performance behavior, which are discussed informally during the performance period and formally during appraisal. Performance is then compared to skill definitions and job tasks, and ratings of performance are jointly developed. This approach measures and guides improvement as the work is done.

**Benefits of a Task-Based
Performance Discussion Forum**

- Structures the performance discussion
- Identifies expectations
- Relates to the job and is legally defensible
- Indicates essential job functions
- Reinforces vision, mission, values, and priorities
- Suggests what to talk about
- Absorbs tension
- Reliably measures performance
- Suggests areas for growth
- Documents what was discussed

A special benefit of the task appraisal strategy is that technical/ job skills and performance skills can provide the linkage between the selection interview and the appraisal form for the same job. For example, in a selection interview, a performance skill such as teamwork would have questions under it. On an appraisal form, the same performance skill could have task statements under it. Review

Exhibit 6.1 to see how the same skill definition can be used to organize both interview questions and job tasks.

A Task-Based Appraisal System

There is a direct relationship between developing a behavior-based interviewing system and developing a task-based appraisal system. This reduces the costs in linking your HR applications because much of the work that was done in creating a structured interview can be used for creating a performance discussion form.

In step 1, a skills analysis provides information on the work context and job requirements for a particular job. Step 2, selection and creation of skill definitions, yields a group of technical/job skills and performance skills that should be used for selection and performance discussion. In addition, the development and use of a task-based appraisal system mirrors the steps taken with a behavior-based interviewing system. This is found in the creation of a performance discussion form (step 3), the observation of behavior (step 4) and rating performance (step 5). We will begin our discussion of the task-based appraisal system with the creation of a performance discussion form and continue through the remaining stages.

Step 3: Developing a Performance Discussion Form

There are two very practical ways to develop a job-related performance discussion form. The simple version is to list the technical and performance skills important for doing a job. The skill definitions then provide the basis for a discussion of examples involving use of the skill.

The more sophisticated approach has twenty or more job tasks organized under the skill definitions. With this approach the skill definitions show the general categories of performance, and the job tasks show exactly what needs to be done. This form is actually a job description that is referred to during the performance period and

Exhibit 6.1. The Use of a Performance Skill to Link Structured Interview Questions and Task Statements for Appraisal.

Teamwork: Able to build a service relationship with internal/external customers by giving a timely response to requests and accommodating cultural differences; contributes to continuous improvement with ideas, suggestions, and effort; avoids talking about team members negatively in their absence; describes possible performance improvements to better meet customer needs.

Interview Questions for Teamwork	*Task Statements for Teamwork*
1. Tell me about a time when you were able to help your team by building a service relationship with an internal customer.	1. Support team efforts in order to build a service relationship with a customer.
2. Describe a situation in which you were able to respond to a request in a timely manner even though odds were against you.	2. Respond to requests in a timely manner to avoid being a "bottleneck" for team performance.
3. Give me an example of a time when you ran a risk of becoming unpopular in order to contribute to continuous improvement.	3. Suggest ways for team members to improve performance to contribute to continuous improvement.
4. When were you sensitive in the way that you offered constructive criticism to a team member?	4. Make sensitive suggestions directly to the person needing the input in order to be clear and direct.
5. Provide an example of a time when you made a suggestion to a work team that improved performance in the eyes of a customer.	5. Make suggestions on work procedures to benefit customers.

serves as a discussion guide during a more formal performance discussion. Performance ratings are made by comparing the job tasks with what was actually done.

Remember that a task statement is more specific than a performance skill. It begins with an action verb, followed by an object and a "to" or "in order to" phrase that explains the reason for the action. For example, look at Exhibit 6.2, which contains task statements for one performance skill for a training consultant. When you create lists of tasks like this, you can get a lot of help from *The Dictionary of Occupational Titles* (U.S. Department of Labor, 1991b; 1993). It contains task statements for over ten thousand jobs.

The big objection to developing a job-specific performance discussion form is time. I can imagine that some part of you is screaming, "I don't have enough time to do all of this detail work for each job." However, there are some things to consider before walking away from the idea. First, you already take time to solve performance problems around you. How much of this time is spent dealing with problems that come up because someone didn't know exactly what was expected? To what extent would you be more effective if you spent less time solving problems that shouldn't have happened and more time avoiding problems before they do happen?

Second, the problem of time needed to develop detailed, job-specific performance discussion forms will be solved by technology. Using an experimental version of job description software, I was able to develop a first draft (unedited) of a performance discussion form in less than an hour. I also created a structured interview for the same job. They both were based on the same six performance skills, but the interview had questions whereas the performance dis-

Exhibit 6.2. A Performance Skill and Task Statements for a Training Consultant.

Tolerance of ambiguity: Withhold action or speech in the absence of important information; deal with unresolved situations, frequent change, delays, or unexpected events.

1. Maintain a flexible scheduling and communications system in order to address changing priorities with a minimum of disruption.
2. Manage conflicting or ambiguous information by confirming (restating) actions to take with others in order to ensure that efforts are properly directed.
3. Adapt to surprise problems with tactical solutions and strategic suggestions to minimize disruption of productivity.
4. Make independent decisions in an unstructured environment in order to efficiently and successfully achieve goals.

cussion form had task statements. Examples of these types of forms may be found in Resource C.

Third, a task-based appraisal should have a high level of defensibility. A study was done of 295 circuit court decisions on performance appraisal between 1980 and 1995 (Werner and Bolino, 1997). It was found that decisions in favor of organizations were more likely with an appraisal system that was based on a job analysis. In addition, the systems were more acceptable when they (1) were accompanied by specific, written instructions, (2) involved multiple raters using a systematic approach, and (3) lead to a review of appraisal results with employees.

The study did not show that the use of a behavioral appraisal was more defensible than a trait appraisal. Apparently, the importance of the distinction between traits and behaviors on appraisal cases has not been effectively communicated in testimony. Instead, the courts tended to make decisions based on the systematic use of corporate due process and an accurate rating process.

 ### Step 4: Systematic Observation Through Behavioral Narratives

A behavioral narrative is a written description of a specific event showing what a person did on the job. It is designed to be completed by a jobholder; however, it may also be completed by a manager who is assessing the jobholder's performance.

A behavioral narrative is very easy to complete, either on paper or with a computer. The jobholder first reviews skill definitions associated with the job. This review helps her see the big picture of how the job fits into the organization and serves as a reminder of the important things to be done. The fill-in-the-blank format of the behavioral narrative form (Exhibit 6.3) makes it easy to describe a performance event in about five minutes.

The details covered on a behavioral narrative form are very important cues and reminders about what needs to be done. For example, in describing a situation, you are asked to describe the

Exhibit 6.3. A Behavioral Narrative Form.

A Behavioral Narrative

Name _____

This performance event occurred at _____ on
                                                      (location)
___ / ___ / ___ at about ___ : ___
  (mo/day/yr)   *(time)*

The task was _____

_____

The action I took was _____
                                    (action verb/object)

_____

(in order to)

My actions were influenced/constrained by _____

_____

They related to our core values and priorities because _____

_____

The outcome was _____
              (describe verifiable results of the action, using numbers if possible)

_____

What I learned from this experience was _____

_____

_____

In the future I will _____
              (describe what you will do if confronted by the same or similar task/problem)

_____

_____

where, when, what, and *how* associated with the problem to be solved. Next, there is a description of hindrances or constraints on solving the problem. Then an action verb is used to describe what was done, the object of the action, and the reason for the action. The form also asks for a description of how the actions were consistent or inconsistent with core values and priorities. Finally, the jobholder describes the outcomes that are associated with the behavior and that reflect the results, learning, and future plans that relate to the task or problem. Each person should complete at least one behavioral narrative once a week.

Some people see behavioral narratives as a way to protect themselves from arbitrary appraisals by managers. However, documentation is a minor benefit of using a behavioral narrative. The behavioral narrative helps the individual carry out self-appraisal with behavior-based language. This means that the behavioral narratives written by the jobholder are probably of more value than those written by the manager.

The primary value of behavioral narratives is that they put an important principle into action: *The best appraisal is self-appraisal.* One of the most important aspects of the process of self-change is to notice the behavior that leads to a less-than-desirable result. For example, to eat less, you need to *recognize* when you open the refrigerator. To stay on course, you need to *detect* overeating before it occurs. An important part of changing one's behavior involves *cuing* on what precedes the behavior in need of change.

Jointly Rate Performance

Open, two-way discussion of performance helps the individual understand what needs to be done to improve performance. Participation builds attention, acceptance, and commitment.

Some would argue that individuals should not be rated, even in a participative format. However, rating an individual's performance is desirable for many reasons. First, it is required by law for some governmental agencies in the United States. Second, the rating of an individual's performance is important for showing a person what he or she needs to do to improve. A third, very practical, reason for rating individual performance is to decide who will keep their jobs during downsizing.

W. Edwards Deming argued that managers should substitute leadership for performance appraisal (Walton, 1991). Performance appraisals can demotivate some people, and individuals are only one component of the performance equation. Work systems and teams are responsible for a very large percentage of performance outcomes and problems. This suggests that managers should give priority to evaluating and improving work systems and teams, not the individuals in the system (Scholtes, 1988).

A similar point was made by a colleague of mine, who found that satisfaction with appraisal systems goes up dramatically when a manager recognizes to the jobholder that there were constraints on performance. Apparently, the recognition of a problem with work systems improves the quality of communication in the performance discussion.

All this would suggest that the rating of individual performance could be more effective by changing the setup of the rating scale. Traditional performance-rating scales treat the individual as the single cause of work outcomes, even though work systems or constraints on performance have a dramatic influence on performance. For example, it is easy to see how a service representative would resent a low rating when it was really a computer shutdown that reduced his ability to solve customer problems. Or think of how a shipping clerk would feel about a low performance rating when there was no truck available for making deliveries.

Many aspects of the work environment, in addition to the person doing the job, enhance or constrain performance. You can address this dilemma by having a performance-rating approach that is shaped like a matrix (Figure 6.1). This enables you to rate each task according to the actions of the individual in relation to the outcomes asso-

Figure 6.1. The Rating Matrix.

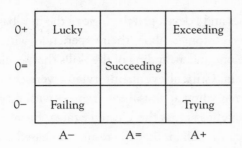

0+	Lucky		Exceeding
0=		Succeeding	
0−	Failing		Trying
	A−	A=	A+

ciated with their actions. In addition, this approach enables the manager and jobholder to focus attention on the actions taken by the jobholder—regardless of the constraints in the work situation.

You can use the rating matrix for skill definitions or for each task statement, thus accounting for the degree to which the jobholders' actions and the outcomes are up to expectations (see Resource C for an example). Before the performance discussion, the manager and the jobholder put a slash mark in the box that best shows the combination of actions and outcomes associated with a particular competency or task. They then discuss the separate ratings in light of the jobholder's actions and the work outcomes.

Here is an example. The jobholder who is "succeeding" on a task, such as "solves problems in order to provide answers to customers," would have a slash mark in the cell that showed both actions (A=) and outcomes (O=) meeting expectation. A jobholder who is "trying" would have a different combination of actions and outcomes. Here the slash mark would show that the individual put forth effort that is above expectation (A+), even though the outcomes (O−) may have been constrained by the work environment.

The rating matrix contributes to performance communications through its separation of individual actions under the control of the jobholder and the outcomes that reflect the contributions of the individual and work systems. This structure will encourage a discussion of the person's actions as partial cause of the results that were gained.

Skills Needed for Task-Based Appraisal

As my colleagues and I developed the logic of the task-based appraisal system, we asked customers about their experiences with appraisal so we could refine our understanding of the skills that would be needed to use the system. Critical-events interviews were conducted over the telephone regarding appraisal experiences with fifty HR professionals in companies across the United States. Because they were all clients, we cannot claim that the results are based on a scientific sample of managers' experiences with performance appraisal. The results enabled us, however, to develop behavioral descriptions of what people did that was effective when giving and receiving performance appraisals. In turn, we gained a better understanding of the skills that managers would need when using a task-based appraisal system.

Altogether, we collected 203 critical incidents. We wrote these incidents on separate pages and organized them into groups that seemed to go together. Then we wrote performance skills that seemed to account for the information covered in the narratives. These skill definitions suggested what should be done before, during, and after a performance discussion.

The performance skills we developed contain some very traditional ideas, such as using a job description to communicate expectations and giving continuous feedback on a daily or weekly basis (Exhibit 6.4). Other comments are so logical that they would barely seem worth mentioning. For example, ask questions to encourage two-way conversation. However, the negative critical events we got in our survey suggested that many appraisers did not do the most basic, logical things.

When these experiences were applied to task-based appraisal, we concluded that a job-related performance discussion form is a necessity for conducting an appraisal that deals with today's concerns. It will also suggest the areas for improvement to be discussed

Exhibit 6.4. Performance Skills for Leading a Performance Discussion.

Preparation and Administration: Communicates expectations with a job description and task statements; gives the jobholder positive and negative feedback on a daily/weekly basis; completes ratings before the meeting and asks the jobholder to do the same; arranges for a convenient time for the performance discussion with at least one week's notice; begins the review at the appointed time and allows sufficient time without interruption in a productive setting; completes forms and forwards them to the proper recipient.

Gain and Manage Information: Observes the performance behavior of the jobholder during the entire performance period; generates behavioral narratives of what the person did in relation to job objectives; avoids subjective impressions and stereotypes when describing performance; develops a representative sample of positive and negative information on what the jobholder actually did; recognizes constraints on performance; does not allow one negative or positive event to influence other ratings.

Develop a Productive Discussion Climate: Asks rapport-building questions; shows listening by restating and paraphrasing what the jobholder says; encourages the discussion of positive and negative information; recognizes personality conflicts/individual adjustment problems; maintains professional language and conduct during the discussion; uses the performance discussion to build/improve the relationship with the jobholder.

Deal with Job Topics: Asks questions and makes comments that relate to specific job tasks under the jobholder's control; avoids subjective impressions and organizational politics; refers to performance skills and task statements during the performance discussion; avoids legally protected/personal topics such as gender, race, color, religion, national origin, age, and disabilities; gathers information to redesign the job as needed.

Involve the Jobholder: Asks questions to encourage two-way communications; recognizes that the perceptions and feelings of the jobholder are important; encourages self-appraisal by asking for self-observations of job performance; uses a participative style that encourages upward communication; avoids generating fear except in matters of discipline and personnel action; asks the jobholder for feedback on the manager's style and the quality of the performance discussion.

in coaching (Chapter Seven). But a form is insufficient by itself to achieve all of the expectations surrounding appraisal. These expectations can be fulfilled only when the people using the system are trained in the skills needed to make the system work. As you will see in Chapter Eight, the necessary training can be implemented by using performance skills to guide the development of instructional objectives.

Summary and Preview

Skill definitions can be used to link performance discussions with selection interviews and an organization's identity. This linkage can be achieved through a task-based appraisal system that uses behavioral narratives to provide a sample of what a person did during a performance period. The comparison of this information to either skill definitions or task statements provides the basis for a meaningful performance discussion. A rating matrix is then used to describe the extent to which the individual's actions and measured outcomes met expectations.

A similar approach can be used for coaching. Here the skills important for doing a particular job are used to describe what the individual needs to do to improve performance. This linkage is achieved by converting phrases in skill definitions or task statements into goal statements that help the individual cue on what to do to meet and exceed performance expectations.

7

Goal-Based Coaching

Change is inevitable; growth is optional.
Michael J. O'Brien, in Personal Mastery Journal

Many years ago, my contact person in a large organization asked, "Paul, do you ski?"

Sensing that something good was about to happen, I responded, "Yes, I do. And not only do I ski, but my nickname on the slopes is 'Death Wish.'"

The client smiled, with the knowing look of a sherpa who was about to guide me to the top of Everest. "We want you to take thirty of our top performers into the mountains for a week-long workshop in individual development. The program will be next spring in Vail, Colorado. Are you available?"

My heart skipped a beat. I could imagine myself gliding down the slopes every afternoon while the participants completed self-assessments and met in small groups. This could be a sweet engagement, I thought.

Then the deal got even sweeter. "Also, I would like for you to stay over for an extra two days to observe as the executives discuss their own goals and objectives. Really, I just want you to be around and become more visible with them. Then you can fly back with them on the corporate jet."

I allowed myself to ascend to about twenty thousand feet before I came to my senses. A little voice in my head said, *This doesn't pass the sniff test. There is no way that you can do a good job under these conditions.* "I have some reservations about this one," I said to my astonished client.

Since then I have rethought this offer many times to resolve the sense of loss that I still feel. My conclusion is that I made the right decision for the wrong reasons. The problem with this development program was not where it was located. It was that the coaching was an event rather than a systematic process that continued over time. There was also a problem with my being the only coach. It would have been more meaningful to develop a system that would help managers become effective coaches and extend their influence over a much longer period.

The nature of coaching systems is being influenced by a change in expectations about coaching. At one time, individuals expected to "be developed," perceiving investments in their careers as being more of a right than a responsibility. Today there is a trend, however, to place the responsibility for career development on the individual, with the organization providing resources and support. Self-directed career programs emphasize the role of the individual in developing *skills that will be needed by the organization* in the future. This emphasis on the individual's role in development is parallel with the organization's assuming more responsibility for developing information systems that help the individual.

Today's coaching system must link individual development to the organization's needs. Logically, you would expect individuals to be coached to

- Learn skills to maintain core competencies and capabilities

- Conform and commit to organizational values and culture

- Perform technical/job tasks well

- Improve performance skills

Not only should coaching be linked to organizational objectives but coaching should also be an extension of appraisal. Areas in need of improvement should be systematically converted to individual development goals.

Systematic coaching is more than a series of steps to follow. Coaching always involves a relationship between two or more people. An individual who learns and grows simply because of being in a learning situation has not been coached. For example, there was no coaching relationship when I taught a college class with 240 students. However, my helping a student one-on-one was a coaching relationship.

There are noticeable differences in the types of coaching relationships that organizations support. The applications model will describe these differences and suggest that goal-based coaching offers the greatest opportunities when developing linked, systematic procedures for helping people grow.

Approaches to Coaching

The applications model reflects different coaching approaches used by organizations. Each approach has something to offer, but, as you will see, goal-based coaching has the advantage of being job related and measurement sensitive; it can also be easily linked to other HR systems.

Motivational Coaching

This approach uses a manager's intuition and interest in all aspects of the person to build motivation. It generates a positive attitude, self-esteem, and confidence. However, there is no systematic approach to defining how the person needs to change, so the advice given may be an off-the-mark opinion of the manager. Coaching sessions are more general than specific and more spontaneous than planned. This approach can generate good feelings but doesn't necessarily lead to behavioral change.

Mentor Coaching

A mentor coaches by being an example of how to act and by sharing advice on what to do. An effective mentor uses experience and wisdom to coach the individual on how to approach his or her work. Much of the effectiveness of this approach can be explained by the jobholder's respect for the mentor's advice. A practical limitation of the mentoring strategy, however, is that it depends on the availability of the mentor. Few organizations have enough wise people to staff an organizationwide mentoring effort.

Personal Growth Coaching

This approach combines systematic measurement with a desire to develop all aspects of the person, whether job related or not. An individual's personality may be profiled to define areas for growth, or the person may receive 360° feedback on a broad range of performance skills. These approaches have appeal because they deal with the whole person, not just a bundle of job-related skills. The downside of this approach is that it becomes less defensible as it moves toward assessment of the whole person instead of measuring job-related skills only.

Goal-Based Coaching

A coach and the jobholder use a systematic process jointly to identify job-related skills in need of improvement. Next they create written descriptions of exactly what is to be learned. The jobholder then observes and rates his or her own behavior and communicates with the coach (Hedge and Borman, 1995). During the discussion and on the job, the coach may serve as a model for the needed skill (Bandura, 1986; Hellervik, Hazucha, and Schneider, 1992). In more

---

Observations on Bear Bryant's Coaching Style

There are times when the high energy around motivational coaching may obscure the fact that goal-based coaching is actually producing the results. This was the case when Thomas Gilbert, a psychologist and member of the Human Resource Development Hall of Fame, observed Bear Bryant's coaching technique (Gilbert, 1988; Zemkie, 1996). Dr. Gilbert saw few displays of inspiration or affection. Instead, he saw Coach Bryant using video cameras to identify players' idiosyncrasies and keeping performance records for every player in every game. This information was as specific as a description of whether the left tackle had his feet in the wrong position or tucked his shoulder in the wrong way. These very detailed observations then became goals for the coach and the players to talk about.

---

formal training, videotaped scenarios or practical examples are used to demonstrate how to use the skill (Latham, 1989).

Realistically, there is no pure approach to coaching. Any coaching system must take advantage of each of the quadrants of the applications model. For example, motivation, mentoring, and personal growth feedback all play a role in goal-based coaching, but its emphasis on remaining work oriented and procedure driven makes it less invasive and more defensible.

The goal-based coaching strategy should contribute to effective learning through its emphasis on observable actions and the verbal rewards for change that are given by the coach. The focus is on what the individual does, not what has happened to the individual. With an emphasis on specific actions, there is a definable target for measurement and meaningful learning objectives.

The Goal-Based Coaching System

The same steps that are used to install a behavior-based interviewing system and a task-based appraisal system also apply to the development of goal-based coaching. This contributes to efficiency in linking all HR systems to the organization's identity.

The same skills analysis that was used to develop a structured interview and a performance discussion form is used in the early stages of developing a coaching system (step 1). The technical/job skills and the performance skills important for the individual's work are then identified and defined as written skill definitions (step 2). Based on job performance, the coach and the jobholder then jointly create a list of development goals (step 3). They may be derived by editing the skill definitions that describe gaps in performance, or they may be based on editing of the task statements that were rated in need of improvement during a performance discussion. With this approach, the jobholder assumes most of the responsibility for observing his or her own behavior (step 4), followed by a self-rating of the extent to which the behavior matches the individual goal statements (step 5).

There is a progressive shift of responsibility from a manager to the individual in interviewing, appraisal, and coaching. The manager is responsible for interview decisions, the manager and jobholder share responsibility for performance ratings, and self-change is the responsibility of the individual. Consequently, much of the coach's job lies in helping the individual create a list of goal statements. The individual being coached will assume the primary responsibility for self-observation and rating.

Creating a List of Coaching Goals

I first learned about goal-based coaching from a clinical psychologist whose offices were next to mine. He called the technique *behavioral medicine* and used it to help adults learn how to eliminate unproductive thoughts. In therapy, he helped his patients learn to

- Recognize situations that preceded bad feelings
- Identify the thinking that caused the bad feelings
- Monitor and then stop unproductive thoughts

Patients kept behavior-based, developmental diaries, with which they monitored their own self-change. In therapy sessions, the patient would review the diary, discuss what was done, and get recognition for progress. It seemed that the approach was success-ful, although it was never really quantified.

Before we go further, I want to compliment you if you noticed that there was a cognitive, not behavioral, component to this ap-proach. Patients were asked to identify and monitor their *thoughts* and actions. The process of *recognizing thoughts* that caused negative feelings played a big role in improvement.

Most managers aren't clinical psychologists, and they don't have the time or training needed to treat jobholders like patients. How-ever, they can take advantage of the behavioral techniques for self-change. A manager can be a better coach by helping individuals observe, describe, and manage their own behavior.

Here is how I applied this approach to the coaching sessions I was retained to do by corporations. Using information from the orga-nization, interview information, and test data, the associate and I created a fill-in-the-blank page for a performance growth diary (Exhibit 7.1). It contained customized performance skills that described what needed to be done on the job to be more productive. These performance skills were the individual's development goals.

The performance skills were aligned with simple rating scales, which the individual used to cue on his or her own behavior every day for two weeks. We then met again, discussed what was learned, and developed a summary of how to use the technique in the future.

My clients came back with more than self-ratings. They gave vivid descriptions of their actions that were different from what they would have done before. These descriptions were very specific: con-fronting an abusive coworker, giving a presentation on a contro-versial topic, and sleeping well despite a stressful experience.

This approach is very limited and expensive if an industrial psy-chologist does all of your coaching. However, it can be effectively

Exhibit 7.1 A Custom Performance Growth Diary.

Here is an example of a page from a performance growth diary for a person needing to be more assertive. Each performance skill was a learning goal that was aligned with a rating scale based on interview and test feedback. The client completed the page every day for two weeks and then returned to share the experiences.

Performance Growth Diary

First, describe an event giving an opportunity for self-assertion.

Situation _____

_____

Actions _____

_____

Outcomes _____

_____

Second, complete a self-assessment of what you did in this situation.

Communicate assertively: Spoke in a level tone; maintained direct eye contact; directly faced the other person; kept hands from face; used affirmative gestures and posture.

1 _____	2 _____	3 _____	4 _____	5 _____
Didn't Try	Attempted Success	Some Success	Good Success	Strong Success

Comment: _____

_____

Express opinion: Stated my opinion when I expected disagreement; said "no" to express disagreement; used phrases like "in my opinion" and/or "I disagree."

1 _____	2 _____	3 _____	4 _____	5 _____
Didn't Try	Attempted Success	Some Success	Good Success	Strong Success

Comment: _____

_____

Make a request: Asked a person to change a service, action, or opinion; stated why I felt the request was important; did not apologize for the request.

1 _____	2 _____	3 _____	4 _____	5 _____
Didn't Try	Attempted Success	Some Success	Good Success	Strong Success

Comment: _____

_____

used by a manager who uses a coaching system that mainly requires the manager to help the individual identify and describe his or her own developmental goals. The effectiveness of the coaching process is then determined by the commitment and skills of the individual.

The Coach Facilitates Goal Setting

A great number of anecdotal and research-based examples show that goal setting enhances performance. Goal setting is a *must do*, not just *nice to do* (Locke and Latham, 1990). The manager has a critical role in facilitating this process. The following three principles apply:

Participation. Developmental goals should be set *by* jobholders, not *for* jobholders. The individual must freely participate in the goal setting. Boundaries may limit the types of goals to be set or funded by the organization. However, management must give up some control to make goal setting work.

Specificity. General goals such as "do the best you can" have less productive results than specific goals. Specific goals need to describe what is to be done and what outcomes are expected. Performance skills and job tasks can be easily converted into specific goal statements.

Challenge. Goals that are easily achieved do not significantly increase performance. Goals that present a realistic challenge, however, are associated with higher levels of performance. Performance skills are more likely to be meaningful goals when they require significant individual effort.

There are several ways to coach a person on writing development goals. At the most general level, the entire performance skill can become a development goal. This approach could be refined by developing goal statements from the brief phrases in a performance skill. Still better, the job tasks that are organized under a performance skill could be converted into coaching goals.

Combine Task Statements to Set Coaching Goals

If you have task statements for an individual's job, it is possible to combine tasks in need of improvement. For example, here are two task statements that reflect room for improvement for a salesperson:

1. Ask fact-finding questions of the customer to clarify concerns and reasons to buy.

2. Give an example of effective service to provide reassurance to the customer following an objection.

The manager and the jobholder combine the two task statements into one goal statement. Notice that much of the goal statement borrows the wording from the task statements.

Ask fact-finding questions following an objection to clarify understanding of the customer's concerns and to select a meaningful service example to describe.

With this approach, a performance discussion centers on job tasks to set coaching goals. The manager coaches the salesperson on questions to ask and service examples to give. In addition, the salesperson uses self-coaching, before, during, and after each sales call.

The Coach Distinguishes Between Types of Goals

It is reasonable to assume that a coach should be prepared to provide information on careers, discipline, and resources. In addition, the coach should help the individual take advantage of the difference between outcome goals and learning goals (Winters and Latham, 1996).

- *Outcome goals* reflect achievable results or outcomes. Set outcome goals when the individual has a task consistent with his or her skill level.

- *Learning goals* address what to learn to reach a more complex goal. Set learning goals for tasks that are demanding for the individual.

This distinction is very important in coaching. Outcome goals relate to objectives for growth that are reasonably simple and short term. These goals might relate to making an immediate change in one's behavior. For example, here is an outcome goal for planning: "Review my calendar in the morning of every work day to make every scheduled appointment on time." A planner can be used to organize time and commitments with a modest amount of effort. Elimination of missed appointments is the outcome.

When dealing with complex or demanding change, learning goals apply. For example, learning how to be a better listener is more complex than regularly using a calendar to make appointments. Here is a learning goal for listening: "Restate and summarize other's comments aloud to discover what another person is communicating." In this case, the individual will learn what is communicated in several situations. Over time, this skill will be refined and developed, based on the individual's experiences in using restatement and summary.

Learning goals are very important in improving relationships. For example, questions to ask when setting relationship goals might be: "What can I learn from your bad behavior to improve our communications? What can I learn about myself to understand what makes you act badly toward me? What can I learn to do to ignore your dislike of me?" Learning goals can help you to better deal with the disappointments that we all experience in our relationships. Someone who gives you emotional pain creates a learning opportunity.

Self-Observation and Self-Rating

As a consultant I coached individuals to set learning goals in a "redemption program" that I used to do. The program was funded by organizations to offer another chance for improvement for jobholders who were close to being fired. The individual was the client, and all that was said was in confidence. Although I was compensated by the organization, it did not receive a report about the person. In each case, the responsibility for behavior and ratings fell completely on the individual.

Here is an example of how my redemption program worked with a hypothetical individual. We'll call him Stan.

Stan was referred to me because he was very vocal about the difference between the organization's culture statement and the behavior of a particular executive. We began by simply talking through Stan's perceptions of the problem. In his opinion, he was simply being caught in company politics. He recognized that he was guilty of saying the wrong thing at the wrong time. But he didn't feel that he should be treated like an outcast.

We proceeded with Stan, completing a battery of tests and a behavior-based interview. We then reviewed the test and interview findings and profiled his performance skills, based on our understanding of the results. We spent several hours describing Stan's behavior.

Next, we agreed on the performance skills that were Stan's learning goals and described them in a performance growth diary. Once a day, Stan wrote a description of what he did in a situation that related to his learning goals. After two weeks we got together and discussed Stan's experiences.

He couldn't stop talking about what he had learned. This approach made him think about what he was doing and saying. Stan recognized that his actions were a major cause of his problems with people at work. But of most importance, he became aware of what he could do to avoid being a victim of politics at work.

The coaching that Stan received from me was totally job related. There are boundaries on what a coach at work may legitimately talk about or try to change. The more obvious limits include a manager's trying to change a person's religion, political affiliation, lifestyle, family commitments, and so on. That part is easy. But what about the gray area in developing people? What topics are clearly in bounds for development in the context of work?

The standard I have used for defining what is appropriate for development can be found in U.S. law. Both the Americans with Disabilities Act and the Civil Rights Act of 1991 provide a standard for determining whether illegal discrimination has taken place. The decisions or procedures in question are evaluated as to whether they are job related and consistent with business necessity.

I believe that this standard should be applied to coaching. Development should not be directed to the whole person but specifically targeted to the person's job-related behaviors. For a manager to coach an assembly-line worker on how to relate more effectively to the sales department is plausible. But to coach the same worker on which values to adopt to have a happy family is off the mark. Coaching and goal setting should be directly tied to job tasks.

Summary and Preview

Goal-based coaching enables a manager to use a systematic, job-related approach to individual development. It begins with the manager describing and modeling work expectations. Once areas for improvement are jointly selected, the manager helps the job-holder convert the phrases in job-related competencies or tasks into goal statements. They are written out by the jobholder for self-monitoring and future discussion.

In the next chapter you will see how competencies can also be converted into instructional objectives for training. These objectives reflect what a person should be able to do after the training and provide the linkage of the organization's core identity to the training process.

8

Objective-Based Training

If you don't know where you are going, it is difficult
to select a suitable means for getting there.
   Robert F. Mager, in Preparing Instructional Objectives

A director of training once asked me to participate in the identification of the learning needs of a large, wealthy organization. As a consultant, I sensed that this golden opportunity was more than a figure of speech. However, I also knew that I would succeed in the long run by maintaining objectivity about the project. So I took off my marketing hat and focused on being of service during our meeting.

I had just written the words "Learning Objectives" on a flip chart when the vice president of human resources came into the room. He was a smart, articulate executive who generated energy in meetings by succinctly describing a problem and then leaving.

On this occasion, he said: "What we have here is a chance to avoid 'The Great Training Robbery.' Define the learning objectives, and we will know how to do a good job."

Needless to say, I was relieved that he was not looking at me when he referred to "The Great Training Robbery." However, I was even more pleased to hear that he clearly supported the idea of developing a training effort based on learning objectives.

The needs analysis that we did resulted in a training strategy that reflected what the different divisions needed their people to learn. Today, however, individual and divisional objectives are not enough. Training must reflect the learning needs important for reaching the business objectives of the whole organization.

Dana and Jim Robinson approach this opportunity by distinguishing between activity training and training for impact (Robinson and Robinson, 1989). *Activity training* is provided in response to requests that emerge in an organization, which may or may not relate to the whole organization's needs. In contrast, *training for impact* is based on a thorough, up-front analysis, yielding learning objectives that relate to the needs of the whole organization—not just the parts.

In this chapter the development of skill definitions is treated as part of the up-front analysis, which will enable us to align training to other HR applications. Specifically, skill definitions that reflect the organization's identity and job requirements will be used to suggest learning objectives. This will be done by expanding a phrase in a skill definition to a series of learning objectives. Each of these learning objectives will have a prefix: "on completion of this instruction a participant will be able to. . . ." Specific learning objectives will be developed from the phrase, with refinements offered by the designer (Mager, 1984).

Approaches to Training

The applications model helps us organize training options around focus and process. Recall (see the figure in the introduction to Part Two) that the horizontal line reflects focus, moving from *person oriented* on the left to *job related* on the right. The vertical line represents *process* and extends from *intuitive* at the top to *procedural* at the bottom. The combination of a structured process and job-related focus is seen as the best way to link training to other HR systems and the organization's identity. This will be reflected as objective-based instruction.

Smile Training

As its name implies, smile training creates good feelings in participants. Training is intuitively directed toward the whole person through special events, motivational speakers, and recognition programs. For example, sending a whole work team to hear a motivational speaker can spark a better level of communication. However, in smile training, participants are recipients of an experience, not active participants in learning. If you need associates to develop new knowledge and skills, another type of training may serve you better.

Hands-On Training

Associates learn through the experience of actually doing the job. This approach combines a job focus with the experience of doing the work. Once called *vestibule training*, factory workers learned their jobs in a vestibule to the side of the assembly line. They performed the same tasks as the workers on the line as part of their training. In its more current form, a new worker first observes the job being done and then develops the skills over time by working next to a more experienced colleague.

Instrument Training

With this approach, the individual gets information about his or her skills based on standardized instruments that have not been customized for the organization or the jobs in it. This includes off-the-shelf competency profiles, personality tests, style inventories, and generic 360° feedback surveys. Although many of these instruments provide important feedback to the individual, they do not directly link to the identity of the organization or job requirements. Feedback is given to the whole person, regardless of job relatedness. In some cases the feedback actually infringes on the privacy of the individual.

Objective-Based Instruction

This approach combines a structured, instructional design with a focus on the specific things to be learned to do the work well. A key to this approach is the development of instructional objectives that identify what is to be learned (Gagné and Medsker, 1996; Mager, 1984; Rothwell and Kazanas, 1992). These objectives are phrased in terms of what the person should be *able to do* after the training (Exhibit 8.1). The learning experience is designed to help participants do what was learned. Emphasis is placed on models of correct behavior, tests for understanding, and rewards for learning.

Each of these approaches has its own merits and frailties. Objective-based instruction, however, offers a systematic way to reinforce organizational identity and strategy. Also, instructional objectives have particular value in describing what needs to be learned to

Exhibit 8.1. Sample Instructional Objectives.

Interviewing Class:
On completion of this class section, you will be able to
1. Identify sources of error and bias in a video of "the typical interview"
2. Contrast the behavioral and trait approaches to interviewing
3. Give examples of trait responses
4. Explain how behavioral information is a good predictor of job performance
5. Gain behavioral examples in the interview

Performance Communications Class:
On completion of this class section, you will be able to
1. Distinguish between examples of essential, nonessential, or non-job-related actions
2. Systematically observe actions to gather representative behavioral information
3. Write a behavioral narrative that will describe performance behavior
4. Use performance questions to identify the causes and constraints of performance

maintain and develop core competencies, capabilities, core values, and priorities.

Accountants Learn Face-to-Face Selling Skills

At one time accounting firms were prohibited by their professional code of ethics from approaching potential clients who were already being serviced by an accounting firm. When these guidelines were updated, one of the big ten accounting firms initiated practice development classes. It identified itself as having an important capability in dealing with mainstream America, including entrepreneurial, high-growth organizations. In addition, it held aggressive targets for the growth of its management consulting services.

A series of learning objectives was set for three classes, which were reflective of professional sales techniques and the core competencies, capabilities, and core values of the organization. Here is a list of objectives involving face-to-face sales skills to be met during the first class.

On completion of this class a participant will be able to

- State the features and benefits associated with services of an entrepreneurial accounting firm
- Make targeted benefit statements about audit, tax, and consulting services for the client with less than $100,000 in revenue
- Explain the benefits of using an accounting firm with extensive experience working with high-growth firms
- Respond to concerns by restatement and a question, fact, or benefit statement
- Request the opportunity to service the potential client

Subsequent classes addressed the challenge of using the skills when there were multiple decision makers and political influences on the decision. After the classes, there was a dramatic increase in the number of calls made. Course evaluations indicated that one of the major benefits of the training was to increase confidence that making calls on potential clients was a professional responsibility.

An Objective-Based Training System

The same series of steps used in developing structured interviews, performance discussion forms, and coaching goals directly translates to the development of objective-based instruction. These techniques are not particularly new for the professionals who work in instructional design. However, we will make a special application of them by systematically linking instructional objectives to the learning needs of an organization and specific jobs within it.

The benefit of this approach is that the structure of a class can be traced to the content of a specific job, including job tasks, and the context of work, including the identity of the organization. Once your performance skills have been developed to meet these standards, they may then become the stimulus for developing instructional objectives.

The Skills Analysis and Creating Skill Definitions

In step 1 of the skills analysis for training, spend additional time in dealing with what jobholders need to learn in order to do the job well. An extra component would be to address job change, anticipating what will need to be learned in the future.

In step 2, skill definitions are developed that suggest the wording of instructional objectives. These skill definitions combine a broad array of information about the organization and individual jobs. A review of Exhibit 8.2 will show what I mean.

Creating a skill definition based on an analysis of the job is hardly a breakthrough in instructional design. However, it is important to take this step to make the linkage of training to other HR systems. In addition, there should be some economies in using the same steps in developing each HR system. One skills analysis should generate enough information to create skill definitions that are used in interviewing, appraisal, coaching, and training.

Exhibit 8.2. Link Mission to Interview Questions, Task Statements, Coaching Goals, and Instructional Objectives.

A phrase from a mission statement	. . . a worldwide leader in quality production, distribution, and delivery of automotive products and services.
A phrase from a performance skill	Quality leadership: Able to use tactful repetition and restatement to influence coworkers to adopt changes in procedures that will continuously improve quality.
An interview question	Give me an example of a time when you were able to use tact and repetition to influence a coworker to put forth extra effort to do a quality job.
A task statement	Restate coworker suggestions on how to improve quality and performance to jointly evaluate possible changes in production systems.
A coaching goal	Restate work team suggestions to pull out different opinions from the group on quality standards.
An instructional objective	On completion of this class, the participant will be able to restate the opinions of others in a team discussion of quality standards.

Developing Instructional Objectives

An instructional objective must be worded in behavior-based language. This means that each instructional objective should describe what a participant is able to do after the training event. The wording should avoid attributes such as "be versatile" and describe instead what a person does who is versatile. Try the exercise in Exhibit 8.3. The training class is then designed to help participants reach the objectives.

For example, I once taught a series of self-assertion classes to help people deal with domineering bosses and coworkers. It was not effective to say that the class objective was to teach participants how to be assertive. It was effective to design a class in which participants showed that they were able to do the things that an assertive person does.

Exhibit 8.3. Distinguish Between Behavior-Based and Attribute-Based Instructional Objectives.

Use a check mark to show that you can distinguish between behavior-based and attribute-based instructional objectives. The correct answers are below.

	Behavior-Based	Attribute-Based
1. Be creative in applying the difference between traits and behaviors.	_____	_____
2. Describe what a person would do when applying organizational values to customer decisions.	_____	_____
3. Ask questions in order to clarify understanding.	_____	_____
4. Understand the difference between informational feedback and action-based feedback.	_____	_____
5. Develop the capacity to adapt to difficult people.	_____	_____
6. Read the steps on the checklist aloud and listen for confirmation prior to take off.	_____	_____
7. Adapt to customer needs by converting features into benefits.	_____	_____
8. Expand the ability to understand and accept a person from a different culture.	_____	_____
9. Restate what was said in order to ensure clear reception of what was said.	_____	_____
10. Become more sensitive to another person's needs for comfort and security at work.	_____	_____

Answers: Instructional objectives 2, 3, 6, 7, and 9 are behavior based.

One of the instructional objectives of the class was to be able to say "no" to inappropriate requests. For example, John was a very nice person who went too far in accommodating others. Because of the instructional objective, he participated in a class exercise in which he practiced saying "no." He was asked to drive another person home and wash his car. He initially replied, "Well, I'm not sure." But after several trials he could assert himself by saying "no" to this and other unreasonable requests. We went from a generality, "be assertive," to a behavior, saying "no."

The systematic conversion of performance skills into learning objectives is very direct. At its simplest level each phrase in the performance skill can be simply restated as a learning objective. A more thorough approach would be to develop several learning objectives from each phrase. Exhibit 8.4 demonstrates exactly what I mean.

There is an opportunity to expand a phrase in a skill definition to explain why the learning is important. Here the instructional objective is nested, containing an objective within an objective.

You can use a nested objective to help associates relate what is learned to organizational identity. In addition, a nested objective reminds the instructional designers to relate the content of the training to organizational identity and strategy.

A nested objective includes "to" or "in order to" after the statement of what is to be learned. This borrows from the approach used to word a task statement in job analysis. Recall that a task statement begins with an action verb followed by an object and a "to" or "in order to" phrase.

Here is a nested objective from an interviewing class that links to an organization's values for respect and honesty to the instruction.

Upon the successful completion of interview training, a participant
   will be able to remain silent after asking a question *to* show
   respect for the individual's need to have time to think of an *honest*, accurate answer.

Exhibit 8.4. Expanding a Performance Skill into Instructional Objectives.
Here is a performance skill on coaching.

Goal-Based Coaching: Show a jobholder how to convert performance skills
or job tasks in need of improvement into goal statements; explain the difference between outcome goals and learning goals, and ensure that the goal
statements reflect learning goals; jointly develop a personal growth diary
containing goal statements and explain how to use it in self-observation;
jointly review a performance growth diary, facilitate descriptions of things
learned, and reinforce productive learning.

Here are some instructional objectives for module one of a class to teach
coaches. Notice that they are an extension of the first phrase in the skill
definition.

On completion of module one, a participant will be able to show a jobholder
how to convert performance skills or job tasks in need of improvement into
goal statements.

1. Explain the importance of setting goals for performance improvement.
2. Interview the jobholder on past performance and appraisal results to
   identify areas of improvement.
3. Explain the difference between performance skills and task statements.
4. Combine performance skills and task statements into accurate descriptions of learning goals for the individual.
5. Gain agreement from the individual that the goal statements are a
   reasonably accurate description of areas for his or her performance
   improvement.

Other learning objectives would come from the other phrases in the competency.

In coaching (Chapter Seven) we discussed the use of outcome
goals when the individual is to perform a task that is consistent with
his or her skills. In contrast, learning goals are used when it is
important to develop new skills. This distinction may be nicely
reflected in an instructional objective. By including a "to" phrase
in a nested objective, it is possible to be very clear about what is to
be learned in relation to the organization and the job.

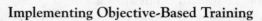 ## Implementing Objective-Based Training

There are many types of training to meet your business
needs. Training magazine lists forty-two training topics, ranging from

new employee orientation, interviewing, listening, and motivation to smoking cessation (Industry Report, 1997). There are twenty-five types of instructional methods, including classroom programs, videotapes, role plays, computer-based training, and virtual reality. Training is provided through one of three sources: in-house, outside supplier, and a combination. This means that there are at least 3,150 ways an organization can use training to meet its objectives ($42 \times 25 \times 3 = 3,150$). With so many opportunities available, the implementation of training needs must be systematic, not anecdotal.

The decision on how to implement training is made even more complex because of the delivery choices that are now available. Recently, training technology has progressed from audio cassettes, video instruction, and digital slide presentations, to the Internet, intranets, and extranets. Along with these opportunities come the challenges of deciding the extent to which the training should be delivered inexpensively, without instructors, classrooms, or travel.

I will not attempt to unravel these mysteries as I discuss training implementation. Instead, I will adhere to the discipline espoused in this book by emphasizing the use of behavior-based skill definitions to link HR processes while reflecting the identity of the organization. To this point there are three examples from the immense number of training opportunities that offer benefits in this arena. They are *training and technology, orientation training,* and *learning contracts*.

Training and Technology

Much of the training to advance core competencies and capabilities and to instruct on technical/job skills can be delivered through computers. As I write, several hundred million dollars of revenue are being generated by companies that teach people things as basic as how to use a word processor or as complex as how to learn new programming languages. In addition, technology is already delivering just-in-time training, and offering thirty-second reminders and minicourses on how to perform very specific tasks, such as wing flap maintenance on a 747.

The combination of training and technology also can be expected to offer new ways to innovate to expand an organization's core competencies and capabilities. For example, a hypothetical record club might plan to develop a core competency around a telemarketing group that will use an Internet customer contact system that enables audio and visual interaction with customers. To develop this function, a vendor is selected to develop the system. The telemarketing group is then taught how to use the system at their work stations by interacting with a trainer who plays the role of a customer. As Internet capabilities expand, the system enables the organization to develop an entirely new type of customer relationship.

Technology can also support instruction that relates to core values. For example, an organization places a great value in employing self-reliant individuals who are actively involved in decision making. To support this value, training is provided through simulations presented on computers that present dilemmas involving values to work teams who respond to the questions presented and discuss them. This training could be more effective and less expensive than traditional classroom learning.

To what extent some form of computer-based training will take the place of the classroom is not clear. A case can be made that technical skills training by computers is faster, cheaper, and better. However, I believe that performance skills training will only be supported by computers. Managers are not likely to master leadership or teamwork without being in a learning situation with other people.

Orientation Training

Orientation training provides an opportunity for introducing new hires to the identity of the organization and showing how it can be carried out in individual jobs. Orientation training is described in *Training* magazine (1997) as being the number one type of training; 92 percent of the organizations surveyed provide it in some form.

Improved orientation training can do a lot to ensure that new hires are prepared to do what is needed to succeed in the organization. For example, here is a learning objective for an orientation class.

Upon the successful completion of orientation training, a participant will be able to explain how the core values of the organization relate to honesty with customers and service policies.

Although many organizations use orientation training to introduce the values and culture of the organization, others use orientation training to describe products and services, pass out booklets on insurance benefits, and review policies. More progressive orientation training can generate a positive first impression of the organization, which alerts new hires to the organization's identity and how it should be fulfilled in doing the job.

Learning Contracts

A learning contract is a written description of what an individual agrees to learn and how an organization agrees to support the learning. It is negotiated between a jobholder and a manager or internal consultant in light of the individual's personal learning objectives and the organization's learning needs.

Learning contracts can be particularly effective in supporting and expanding the core competencies and capabilities of the organization. An individual negotiates the time or resources needed to learn a set of technical/job skills needed by the organization. The manager has evidence of the jobholder's motivation to learn and the right to monitor and measure the learning.

The learning contract has value in helping individuals direct their own learning according to their own interests. When the individual is free to choose what to learn, it is more likely that he or she is committed to the learning process.

Evaluate Training

When there is a discussion of training effectiveness, the conversation will inevitably move to "the four levels" described by

Kirkpatrick (1994). As shown in Exhibit 8.5, the levels range from taking the reactions of participants to measuring the results of the instruction. Each of these levels can measure the relevance of the training to the organization's needs.

An instructional objective suggests a way to measure learning. It is an important component of objective-based instruction because it communicates what will be learned and leads to a test of the learning. For example, here is an instructional objective that relates to this chapter.

Exhibit 8.5. The Four Levels of Training Evaluation.

The four levels represent a progressively more difficult sequence of strategies for training evaluation. The complexity and potential benefits of the evaluation strategies increases with each stage.

Level 1—Reaction (simple to do). This level measures the effectiveness of training based on the reaction of participants. Reactions are typically taken through a course evaluation that is completed immediately after the class. Reactions are valuable because they suggest program improvements, give trainers feedback, and document the perceived value of the training.

Level 2—Learning (relatively simple to do). Effectiveness is measured by the extent to which the individuals acquired the knowledge or skill that was taught in the training. This can be done through such things as a pre- and posttest of learning, demonstration of skills acquired, or measure of attitude change.

Level 3—Behavior (difficult to do). Many people would argue that the purpose of training is to change behavior of participants on the job. However, it is important to recognize that the training may have been well designed, but the individual did not want to change or was encouraged not to change by the work situation.

Level 4—Results (very difficult to do). The highest level of training evaluation is conducted when improved performance or decreased cost is caused by training. For example, did revenue go up after a sales training class? This level of evaluation is professionally challenging because it is difficult to show that training is the only cause of improved performance.

On completion of this chapter, you will be able to explain how to word an instructional objective to reflect an organization's mission.

Notice that this wording describes exactly what you should be able to do. It is possible for someone to see and hear you demonstrate that you have learned the skill. For example, you might learn how to meet this objective by carefully reviewing the information in Exhibit 8.2. Then you might explain it to another person. A rating of your explanation on accuracy and clarity would provide evidence for your learning.

Here is another instructional objective for this section.

On completion of this chapter, you will be able to distinguish between instructional objectives written in behavior-based language and training objectives written in attribute-based language.

Look at the self-test entitled "Distinguish Between Behavior-Based and Attribute-Based Instructional Objectives" (Exhibit 8.3). You can use the test to assess the extent to which you are able to meet the instructional objective. If you were unable to make the distinction, you could improve on your learning by reviewing Chapter Three. This makes the learning process incremental; you are able to learn and test until it is clear that the learning has been achieved.

Summary and Preview

You can use behavior-based performance skills to help you develop instructional objectives that reflect the skills to be learned in doing particular jobs in a particular work context. This enables you to link instructional objectives to the organizational identity directly, including core competencies, capabilities, core values, and priorities.

Chapter Nine will present practical examples of how core competencies, capabilities, core values, and priorities have been linked through skill definitions in both U.S.-based and international businesses. Applications will be described with interview training, performance communications, use of an intranet for skills analysis, and large-scale campus recruiting.

9

Examples of
Competency Applications

Everyone has a great idea until the burden of
implementation falls on them.

Robert Santangelo

There is a big difference between being a spectator and being a
performer. Spectators look—performers do. For instance, I
really like to hear a good rhythm and blues singer. I always thought,
"I could learn to sing like that if I just would take the time to practice." So I brushed off our karaoke player and practiced with a John
Lee Hooker soundtrack. This was a big disappointment! But it was
also a learning experience. Because I am not very good, I appreci-
ate even more those who really can sing.

So it is with building robust competencies. A few star performers
deserve recognition. These are organizations who have been creative
and systematic in the ways they have reflected core competencies,
capabilities, core vision, and priorities in their HR practices.

The following examples are from organizations in different
industries, each with its own problems and challenges. You will see
how corporate identity is reflected in selection interview training.
Then you will see how vision and values were reinforced in self-
directed career planning. Next, there is the integration of critical
organizational competencies into an existing interviewing system
to develop an organizationwide selection strategy. Finally, tangible

results are presented using skill definitions to reinforce selection objectives internally and to standardize large-scale college recruiting. In each case, HR applications are used to communicate and address important business needs. You will see what others have done to move from being a spectator to being a star.

Federal Express: Integrating the Company Philosophy into Diverse Cultures

Federal Express is a premier transportation company with international offices in 211 countries. Its 40,000 couriers deliver 2.5 to 3.0 million packages daily, based on the support of about 1,500 pilots flying more than 563 jet aircraft. At the time of the publication of this book, Federal Express is about an $11 billion company that is known for a unique combination of entrepreneurial spirit and sophisticated work systems.

One of the reasons for the success of Federal Express is its corporate philosophy, developed by founder Fred Smith more than twenty-five years ago. Its philosophy is powerful because of its simplicity and focus: *People, service, profits*. By putting people first, the organization has achieved one of the most studied and acclaimed human resource systems of the twentieth century. The net result is a committed workforce that faces the challenge of high performance, not the worry of unemployment.

The service offered by the organization is legendary. This is not by accident. Service indicators regularly show how well the company is doing in the eyes of its customers and those who provide the services. This builds the profits that are necessary for staying in business. No profits means no capital for growth and no jobs.

The strength of the Federal Express philosophy offered unique challenges as it expanded its worldwide operations. Larry McMann is responsible for the training operations in the European headquarters in Brussels, Belgium. Integration of the company philosophy into the diverse cultures and personnel standards of Europe provided a unique challenge. The company was faced with the need to be firm about the way it does business while showing respect for the cultures in which it operates. Doing business in Europe means that every day you are a guest in another person's home. You have to show respect, even when you don't know all of the rules.

One of the problems they faced was the installation of a structured selection system with international employees who were accustomed to making decisions on an intuitive basis. In addition, different countries have very different standards and sensitivities about race, gender, color, religion, national origin, disabilities, and age. These different approaches to diversity often differed from the Federal Express philosophy, thus making it more difficult to standardize selection interviews and make sensitive decisions.

Federal Express addressed these issues by adapting the Behavioral Interviewing training materials to international needs. International managers reviewed all examples, graphics, and modes of expression so as to avoid even a slight offense. Information that could possibly create discomfort was retained only if it was consistent with the company's philosophy. For example, videotaped examples of women in positions of authority over men were retained.

Skill-building exercises were reviewed to ensure consistent application of the service philosophy at Federal Express. For example, one skill-building exercise in the generic program used the following skill definition.

Interaction: Able to communicate with others in a warm and helpful manner while simultaneously building credibility and rapport.

The skill definition was edited for the exercise to reflect the people and the service components of the corporate philosophy.

Interaction: Able to communicate with customers in a timely and helpful manner; gives priority to the customer's needs over all other aspects of work; thanks customers for the opportunity to serve.

The customization of the generic skill definition made the training materials more representative of the Federal Express philosophy. For example, the company's emphasis on profits was expressed in the estimated costs associated with possible selection mistakes.

Each of these ideas provided a way to reinforce the corporate philosophy as participants in a training class learned how to use the behavioral interviewing system. This meant that training was able to reinforce the corporate philosophy and identity while building interviewing skills.

Grainger Parts: Developing a Model to Integrate HR Systems

Grainger Parts (GP), based in Northbrook, Illinois, is a division of W. W. Grainger, Inc. It provides repair and replacement parts for Grainger's catalogue products and other commercial and industrial equipment. Recognized for its superior customer service, GP is in a constant state of self-evaluation and improvement.

In the fall of 1996, Barbara Chilson, who is now the president of GP, initiated a cross-functional task force with the goal of developing HR systems to support the organization's vision and values. It made the recommendation to senior management that GP develop a single competency model to integrate all human resource systems and support the accomplishment of GP's vision. After due diligence, the management team elected not to buy an off-the-shelf competency model but to build one with the help of novations consultants who were highly experienced in developing competency systems. Together, they identified the key behaviors of GP's high performers, as well as the future behaviors necessary for accomplishing GP's long-term strategic objectives.

The first step of the project involved the description of GP's work context by converting the organization's strategy into a series of core values and priorities that would describe the context of work for all jobs in the organization. There was heavy participation in the process, with the development team using a collaborative methodology to build broad-based employee commitment during the data-gathering, development, and validation phases of the project. An aggressive two-month schedule produced a competency model that included ten characteristics of the organization's core values and priorities (Exhibit 9.1).

The broad competency model of the organization was then linked to the Four-Stages™ Model, originally developed by Gene Dalton and Paul Thompson (1993). These Harvard professors discovered that individuals who remained highly productive throughout their careers approached their work in very different ways,

Exhibit 9.1. The Ten Core Values and Priorities of Grainger Parts.

Analysis and decision making: Processes information for the purpose of making informed decisions to accomplish work objectives.

Flexibility: Adapts positively to changes in direction, priorities, schedules, and responsibilities.

Planning and prioritizing: Organizes and monitors work to ensure that goals, objectives, and commitments are met.

Teamwork: Works collaboratively and cooperatively in groups for the purpose of achieving shared objectives consistent with GP's mission and individual work goals.

Relationship building: Builds and maintains productive relationships with others who share a commitment to the achievement of GP vision and goals.

Know the business: Demonstrates an understanding of GP's and Grainger's mission, strategies, and competitive environment by using this knowledge to achieve business objectives.

Developing self and others: Recognizes and acts on the need to continually develop professional and organization competencies in self and others, consistent with the needs of GP.

Innovation: Initiates and supports new ideas and processes.

Personal commitment: Takes personal responsibility for achieving individual and team objectives, consistent with job expectations.

Job expertise: Demonstrates the technical, professional, and job-specific knowledge required to be proficient in one's current assignment.

depending on the stage in which they were operating. The stages were as follows:

Stage One: The Assistant Stage. At this level the individual is under close supervision and direction. Individuals at this stage are expected to accept supervision and stay in the boundaries of their responsibilities. If they learn well at this stage they advance; if not, they may remain in the organization in this role.

Stage Two: The Individual Contributor. Self-direction and expansion of personal responsibility are characteristic of this level. Peer relationships and high proficiency in their work discipline become more important as they progressively work in technologies that are central to the mission and strategy of the organization.

Stage Three: Contributing Through Others. This stage doesn't necessarily mean managing other people. Recent research from ten technical organizations shows that nonsupervisors outnumber supervisors five to one in Stage Three. Stage Three contributors have discovered how to have a broader impact in the organization through being a coach, project leader, or internal consultant.

Stage Four: Leading Through Vision. Individuals at this level do such things as shape the direction of the organization, make important organizational decisions, and sponsor people who might fill future key roles in the organization. Most people in this stage are in management roles; however, many innovators and internal entrepreneurs have no direct reports.

The transition from stage to stage is far from automatic. It requires taking a new approach to one's job—in effect, renegotiating one's role in the organization. Such role renegotiations—called novations—require a change in relationships, tasks, perspective, knowledge, skills, and abilities. However, an organization cannot "novate" you. You have to do that yourself by taking a different approach to the way you accomplish work.

The Four-Stages Model was linked to each of GP's ten competencies by identifying the important behaviors at each stage that relate to the competency. For example, Exhibit 9.2 shows how the four stages relate to analysis and decision making. Similar models were developed for the other nine competencies.

The formal communications roll-out began in early 1997, supported by a three-day "coaching and development" workshop for the entire management team. Managers were then asked to begin "speaking the language" of competencies with all employees and to communicate the time frames for the phased implementation. For example, career development training for all employees began in early 1998, supported by participants receiving 360° feedback based on the behavioral descriptions contained in the new competency model. In addition, monthly supervisory roundtables offer a forum to share success stories and seek ways to overcome obstacles. Collectively, these initiatives reinforce the language of the GP culture and priorities.

The strongest endorsement of the project came from Rick Adams, GP's president at that time. "Although I fully support the formal roll-out of the competency model, the real payoff comes when we naturally incorporate GP's competency framework into our day-to-day activities." He added, "I'm personally doing that for myself, and I'm encouraged that others are doing it as well."

Caliber Logistics: Using a Competency-Based Approach to Selection

Caliber Logistics, based in Hudson, Ohio, is a contract-logistics company that provides services related to managing transportation or materials across the entire supply chain. Formed in 1989, it is a relatively young company that has earned the reputation as a dynamic, high-growth business. Like many organizations today, its future is molded by its ability to hire outstanding employees. This

Exhibit 9.2. The Relationship of Analysis and Decision Making to the Four-Stages Model.

Analysis and decision making: Processes information for the purpose of making informed decisions to accomplish work objectives.

Stage One: Helping and Learning

- Knows where and how to get information for decision-making purposes
- Demonstrates common sense in day-to-day assignments
- Pays attention to basic details and is accurate when processing, handling, or interpreting data
- Thinks before acting
- Seeks help when having difficulty interpreting data or when facing difficult situations that impact others
- Uses basic mathematical analysis to solve problems
- Is learning to see patterns, trends, or missing pieces when looking at and evaluating information

Stage Two: Personal Leadership

- Takes initiative in identifying and acting on opportunities and problems
- Makes well-reasoned trade-offs
- Keeps work moving despite uncertainty
- Uses both logic and intuition when evaluating options
- Thinks ahead to the implications of decisions and actions
- Secures relevant information from different sources to solve nonroutine problems
- Makes decisions in light of a "big picture" perspective
- Integrates pieces of data from different sources into a logical and coherent structure
- Uses accepted GP/Grainger models of data analysis and measures of success
- Exercises sound judgment

Stage Three: Local Leadership

- Shares data with others to help them make informed decisions
- Makes sound, informed decisions, particularly under time pressure in nonroutine situations
- Coaches others on how to incorporate intuition into decision analysis
- Clarifies complex data in situations so that others can comprehend, respond, and contribute
- Assists others in interpreting subtle cues/messages or ambiguous information
- Encourages others to see and try different approaches in complex situations

Stage Four: Organizational Leadership

- Identifies sources of strategic information that improve the analysis of complex situations for others
- Identifies and helps to remove ambiguous, ill-defined, complex problems and processes that cross organizational boundaries
- Establishes the overall framework and context for decision making
- Communicates the importance of clear thinking (both critical and intuitive) in all jobs through GP
- Provides an organizational perspective that others can use to align their decisions with the GP vision and business objectives
- Fosters an organizational culture that promotes ethical decisions

led management to ask, "What makes employees competent in this business?" and "How could Caliber make sure that these competencies were identified, recognized, developed, and rewarded?"

The process of answering these questions started Caliber on a journey that eventually involved the entire company and invited a systematic review of the company's HR systems and management approach. Gay Williams, in instructional design, saw how management immediately grasped and appreciated the concepts behind a competency-based approach to selecting employees. Management also saw the benefits of using competencies to link HR systems, including performance management, training, and development. This understanding and commitment was very important to the project, according to Williams, because management was involved from the beginning.

The first step involved developing a selection process based on competencies, with a particular focus on selection for key positions. This began with a pilot focus group made up of the company's leadership team. The group was to help define standards for selection; the outcome was the identification of six critical competencies for the entire organization. These competencies reflected Caliber's criteria for attracting employees who are very customer, team, and systems oriented. The competencies were:

1. *Communication:* Able to talk with customers, make presentations, listen carefully to others, and verbally influence others regularly; able to spend a large amount of time writing, editing materials, documenting work clearly, and reading reference materials

2. *Development of subordinates:* Able to provide challenging assignments, constructive feedback, recognition, and rewards; help others deal positively with mistakes, address performance variances, implement staff development plans, ensure cross training, and promote from within

3. *Systems and process orientation:* Able to use systems thinking to anticipate consequences and prevent problems; comply constructively with written or unwritten rules; use detailed procedures or previously established techniques, conform to standards so systems run smoothly, and maintain consistency

4. *Customer orientation:* Able to ensure that customers know what to expect and keep customers informed; project customers' long-term needs; be resourceful enough to meet complex needs; recover from service failures, make customers feel important, and exceed their expectations; create customer-orientation in one's work group

5. *Partnership:* Able to strategize with customers; manage subleties of change such as timing, politics, or information about decision makers; maintain responsiveness to customers and foster their reliance; succeed in an ambiguous-role environment, provide service within bounds of relationships, and meet customers' needs while meeting own company's needs

6. *Team orientation:* Able to work with people in such a manner as to build high morale and group commitments to goals and objectives; cooperate with team members and do a fair share of teamwork

These organizational competencies were then integrated into a larger system of individual competencies that would enable interviewers to develop job-related interviews reflecting the broad context of the work, as well as specific job content. Each question was designed in the behavioral format described in Chapter Five. Training materials were then developed that included participant manuals, exercises, and leaders' guides.

The next step involved the certification of twelve HR representatives to conduct the training throughout the organization. They then used the materials to conduct training at their own convenience in the United States and Europe. Each class was evaluated by surveying participant reactions immediately after the class. "The response has been overwhelmingly favorable," says Lynette Huler, Caliber's manager of training and organization development. "Managers are telling us that they've never received such good information from candidates before."

Now Caliber is taking steps to analyze all current positions to identify the essential competencies involved in each job. Williams expects to complete this project, which affects three thousand employees, by year's end. There is discussion of including the entire competency-based selection system in the company's intranet.

"We've seen that the competencies that Caliber had previously identified keep coming up again and again in everyday language. This indicates that the competencies are truly indicative of what it take to be successful at Caliber," said Behavioral Technology's Tracy Tedesco.

Much work remains to be done. "We've developed a systems map of all HR development activities that affect the life cycle of employees, from initial recruitment on," said Patrick Manion, vice president for human resources. "We expect to systematically link competencies to all our HR systems, and to the technology that supports the HR effort."

Deloitte & Touche: Refining a Selection Process

Deloitte & Touche, an international professional services firm with over twenty-five thousand people in the United States, has enjoyed exceptional financial growth during a business period that saw a trend in mergers and acquisitions of professional services firms. Attention to quality and performance standards has paid off with national recognition in both media and professional circles as well as an impressive client list of Fortune 500 companies.

The growing market for the firm's service capabilities increased the demand for highly qualified people, both experienced and entry level. Consequently, the recruiting targets of the firm adapted, with candidates being sought from a variety of disciplines and educational profiles.

In prior years the firm had a very successful track record of recruiting at colleges nationwide. However, the new mix of skills and experience required were factored into its continuous refinements on its selection process. The following steps were taken:

- Desired skills and competencies were reviewed, based on client needs.

- Focus groups of partners, principals, and associates systematically identified critical skills for the future.

- Structured interviews were redesigned to help interviewers efficiently gain information about critical skills.

- Training was provided to recruiting directors and interviewers to ensure consistent use of the process.

The structured interviews reflected the core competencies, capabilities, core values, and priorities of the organization and its jobs. Included in the shared values of the firm were dedication to clients, recognition of the importance of people, commitment to quality, a sense of partnership/teamwork, and financial success. These shared values and practice standards articulated what they respect as an organization and how they operate.

Preliminary training was conducted to assess the quality of the Behavioral Interviewing approach and to solicit feedback from partners. Their participation in the training involved a skills analysis that refined their existing model and clarified the skill set for success in new jobs. This was the key for building commitment and designing selection that was consistent with the organization's strategic perspective. A positive outcome of this step was partner acceptance of the interviewing technique.

Forty-eight trainers were certified to teach the Behavioral Interviewing seminars. They then delivered the training to more than six hundred interviewers over an eight-week period. The result? Participant buy-in was high. They liked the structured approach, which made their interviews more efficient and productive.

The implementation of the interviewing process was sensitive both to client needs and to profession trends that would have an impact on the recruiting and selection of capable, service-oriented professionals. It was begun at a time when the firm was recruiting large numbers of entry-level college graduates while also courting many candidates with professional work experience.

Interviewers solicited feedback from student candidates at more than three hundred colleges on the effectiveness of the approach. Students believed that this type of interview allowed them to better present their experiences and skills as compared to other types of interviews.

Deloitte & Touche will continually reassess its selection process to meet changing business needs. Plans include a more structured approach to follow-up interviews conducted in the firm's offices, updating training for new interviewers to include customized Behavioral Interviewing questions, and enhancing the measurement of overall results as they relate to performance and retention.

Summary and Preview

This chapter has described how performance skills and competencies were applied to a variety of human resource needs in different industries and countries. In each case performance skills were developed by using a systematic procedure, behavioral language, and a job-related approach. The examples showed that there are just a few rules and a lot of potential applications.

If you plan to apply competencies to your organization, you probably have questions. The Epilogue anticipates some of your questions and offers practical suggestions on how to resolve them.

Epilogue: Answers to Common Competency Questions

You cannot step twice into the same river.

Heraclitus

One thing you don't want to miss in your lifetime is the Agora in Athens, Greece. In Greek, *Agora* means "marketplace." The name comes from the open space beneath the Parthenon that was a site of commerce and government more than 4,500 years ago. It has been excavated over the last hundred years or so, exposing the place where ancient Greek philosophers—including Socrates himself—once walked.

The Agora is probably the place where learning by asking questions was first applied with rigor. The advocates of this approach were said to be part of the *peripatetic school,* so-called because learning came from walking about, asking questions, and discovering answers.

This chapter is written in the spirit of the Agora. It deals with questions you may have about how to build and apply robust competencies. Although you have probably absorbed the key ideas of this book, you may have lingering questions—if not objections—that you would like me to deal with.

Each of the following questions has really been asked of me. Many have come up in the workshops I have led, but a substantial number come from casual conversation with people at conventions and professional meetings. Some of the questions have an academic perspective. But all of my comments are offered from a practical standpoint.

Question 1: I am proud of my skill in using my "gut feeling" and experience in making decisions. But you seem to downplay these skills with your emphasis on a structured process. Why?

I believe that some people do have great intuitive powers. And you may be one of them! However, I am equally sure that many of your coworkers do *not* have strong intuitive powers. In my own experiences, I can think of too many people I have worked with who had very little insight about the motivations, personality, or skills of others.

Organized work efforts must accommodate the many who are *not* very effective in using their intuitions. Your organization should have a structured process in place to help people agree on issues such as the level of skill offered by a job candidate. Being able to use a systematic process is very important for being an effective member of a selection team, because you must be able to explain your reasoning to others. In addition, a system will help individuals avoid the use of stereotypes and snap judgments in decision making.

Ironically, I suspect that the people in your organization who are skilled with their intuitions can learn a great deal from the use of a structured process. Think of it like this: Using a structured procedure for gathering information helps feed your intuitive understanding of others. By knowing what you are responding to, you can assess how you make intuitive decisions. This assessment can open you up to new learning rather than allow you to fall into an ego trap of assuming that you don't need to learn new techniques.

Question 2: Why can't I just get a list of competencies and start using them?

You can. It is certainly better to have a clear understanding of what you are going to measure or manage than to have a fuzzy feeling about what you like or dislike about a person.

Behavioral Technology, Inc. has provided lists of performance skills linked to interview questions in our own Behavioral Interviewing Seminars and SkilMatch® software. We estimate that companies have used these performance skills, without editing, on millions of structured interview and performance-discussion forms.

Even though we urge individuals to edit skill definitions in light of their job requirements, we know that it is easier to just use the prewritten competency and the questions or tasks linked to it. Even if it is generic, a competency can contribute to reliable and valid measurement and to effective decision making. However, there is a real benefit from developing your own skill definitions. You are able to communicate your own organizational identity. You can repeatedly emphasize exactly who you are and how you do business each time a form is used.

In addition, I've stressed the importance of participation throughout this book. Participation in developing your core competencies, capabilities, values, and priorities may give you a greater payoff than using an already developed system. Your organization's skill in getting involvement through teams with specific tasks to achieve may offer you a great competitive advantage in the marketplace, which is very important for any well-run business.

Question 3: I believe people do have important attributes that they use to get a job done. In fact, I think personality traits and intelligence are attributes that can predict most areas of job performance. Why do you downplay the use of attributes?

You are exactly right. Personality tests and intelligence tests can predict job performance (Barrick and Mount, 1991; Tett, Jackson, and Rothstein, 1991; Hunter and Hunter, 1984). Regardless of whether people agree with this research, the practical question remains of whether you can use these predictors effectively on a broad scale in an organization. Here are two questions to ask yourself:

Are the tests reliable and valid? Evidence for reliability and validity is best judged by strict professional guidelines (Society for Industrial and Organizational Psychology, 1987; Uniform Guidelines on Employee Selection Procedures, 1978; American Educational Research Association, American Psychological Association, and National Council on Measurement in Education, 1985). Typically, this evidence is provided in a way that is open to public scrutiny. It is published in professional journals and presented in papers at conventions. If the information is proprietary, it can be made available through expert witnesses in a courtroom.

Do you have the professional support for a testing program? In my opinion, a professional staff for maintaining a testing program should include people who have had graduate training in psychometrics, tests, and measurements. This staff should control who has access to the test questions and scoring procedures. They should supervise the administration and interpretation of test results. In some cases, a test publisher or consultant can give you the support you need. But you should not use a testing program for selection without qualified professional guidance.

The beauty of behavior-based interviewing, appraisal, coaching, and training is that it applies the principles of good measurement in a very practical way. Most people in your organization can learn how to conduct a structured interview, but many cannot use a personality or intellectual profile to assess a candidate's employability. That's why I think the behavioral approach is more practical for broad use in most organizations.

Question 4: What benefits could an organization expect to get in light of the costs associated with linking HR systems to organizational identity?

The answer to this question really depends on your organization's needs. If you have a need to reduce ambiguity, the written definition of skills can help through reinforcing your vision, mission, values, and culture. If you have defined your organization's core competencies, capabilities, core values, and priorities, management is better able to give strategic direction. Skill definitions also clarify standards for selection, performance, coaching, and training.

When standards are clarified there is an opportunity to support quality efforts. Standards are defined through the participation of teams of job experts who aggressively question practices and processes. Even if your organization has no quality initiative, when you pull teams together to define technical/job skills and performance skills, they will naturally begin to question standards, execution, and teamwork. Along this line of thinking, the linkage of HR systems to an organization's identity provides an opportunity for meaningful participation and goal setting.

Question 5: How much time is required in training to effectively install competencies in an organization having one thousand full-time employees?

The American Compensation Association (1996) surveyed organizations regarding the development of competency/performance skill models. There were tremendous variations in the time required to generate and implement the projects; 51 percent of the respondents reported needing from nine to fifteen months. The greatest amount of time (40 percent) was spent in developing the model; much less time (17 percent) was spent in implementation and planning.

The same survey reported the amount of time spent in training at the employee level, manager level, and executive level. Half-hour sessions were the most frequent approach used for individual contributors (35 percent) and executives (30 percent). Managers received more instruction; 30 percent attended a half-day session, 10 percent received a full-day session, and 26 percent attended multiple days of training.

Because there is no clear "how to" when it comes to training associates on the use of competencies and performance skills, it is impossible to say how much time is actually required. The big variables are how participative your organization already is, how capable your training staff is, and how complex your model is.

With optimal conditions, I cannot imagine it taking less than two hours of training time for each associate to be able to refer to your competency/performance skill definitions and give an explanation of their practical meaning. When the learning situation is not in your favor, it would probably take six to eight hours per associate to introduce your model with some reasonable level of acceptance and buy-in.

Question 6: Why do you think computers will make the use of competencies and performance skills easier? How can we use computers to help us take full advantage of our model?

If designed correctly, a database can make using your model a delight. Without computers, a competency model can become a nightmare of detail.

Performance skills are strong candidates for computerization because they provide the linking point for HR applications. For example, someone wanting to use the performance skill for *teamwork* could select from prewritten interview questions, task statements, coaching goals, and instructional objectives. The computer retrieves and organizes the information for the user.

Once the performance skills important for a particular job are identified, the user may then be able to use a stand-alone computer or connect to an internet/intranet to select from banks of prewritten interview questions, task statements, coaching goals, and instructional objectives. For example, a team may want to develop a structured interview and a performance-discussion form for a new role. It could consult the banks of prewritten questions and task statements and use the computer system to develop the particular interview and performance discussion form required by the job.

Question 7: How can I use skill definitions to coach myself to get a better job?

Performance skills can be converted to learning objectives. Once you identify what you need to do to change jobs, you can plan for your learning. This knowledge can also benefit your current employer. If you develop a clear statement of the core competencies, capabilities, core values, and priorities that need to be developed and maintained in the future, you should be able to think of your career development as a series of learning targets that help your current employer reach its objectives.

Performance skills can help you prepare for the job interviews that you take. As I described in *Get Hired!* (Green, 1996), you can anticipate interview questions based on job requirements. This enables you to showcase your skills honestly by giving examples of things that you did that demonstrate how well you can do the new job.

In some cases, a close review of your own performance skills may cause you to reject a job that on the surface seems "better." It may be better for some people, but not for you. If the job requirements don't match what you are willing to do, or can do, then look for another opportunity.

Question 8: What we call our core competencies are very different from your definition in Chapter Two. Is it okay for us to use our own definition of a core competency?

By now this book has made it painfully obvious that I think it best to use the term *core competency* when you are using the term the way Prahalad and Hamel (1990) used it originally. Recall that a core competency is technical and unique, developed over a nontrivial period, and able to provide a competitive advantage. See Chapter Two to refresh your memory of this definition, as well as the meaning of *capability*, *core value*, *priority*, *technical/job skill*, and *performance skill*.

I suspect that some dislike my introducing the term *performance skill* as a substitute for an individual competency. There are many smart people who use the term *competency* when referring to a person's skills. However, I prefer to use the word *skill* when talking about what a person is able to do. It is valuable to distinguish clearly an individual's skills from an organization's core competencies, capabilities, core values, and priorities. It is also desirable to make an HR system as skill oriented as possible. It is easy to use behavioral language to describe skills, and they are less expensive to validate than abilities or personality.

Question 9: Please explain again exactly how you use behavioral language to link HR processes.

Behavioral language can link HR processes at a content level and a process level. Content linkage involves using the same or very similar words, phrases, and concepts in more than one HR application. For example, a competency used as part of a structured interview could also be directly reflected in a performance discussion form, coaching goals, and instructional objectives.

HR processes are also linked through the behavioral emphasis on observation, description, and cautious inference. These components are found in each HR application. Here is how:

- Observation is carried out in selection interviews, performance discussion, coaching, and training. Here the emphasis is on paying attention to what is done rather than to one's feelings and intuitions.

- Description is used in taking interview notes, writing narratives for performance discussion, identifying what needs to be done for improvement, and stating what new skills were demonstrated in a classroom.

- Inferences are made in interviews, appraisal, coaching, and training by comparing what was done with the skill definitions that serve as criteria for measurement and objectives for guidance.

The combination of content linkage and the process of using the behavioral approach offers a powerful alternative when aligning individuals with the organization in a profitable and fair manner.

Question 10: You repeatedly emphasize measuring an individual's job-related skills instead of all of the competencies or skills that he or she may have. This makes the development of a competency model much more complicated. It seems simpler to build a model to measure all of a person's competencies and skills, regardless of the job that is being done. Why don't you recommend the simpler way?

The most obvious answer here is that your ability to defend your competency system begins with the extent to which decisions are based on job-related information. Whole person measures generally do not meet that standard. In addition, I don't believe that the broad competency measures are simpler to use. The more that a competency measure is behavioral (and job related), the easier it is to make observations, descriptions, and inferences about a person's performance.

There is also the question of relevance. When you measure the general qualities of a person, you are identifying individual characteristics that may direct attention away from the job to be done. Doesn't it make sense that a competency system should be much more directed at improving performance than at improving people?

The use of broad competency measures is more acceptable when considering the knowledge worker. Here we have a person whose broad skills may be of benefit, even when they are not required in the current job. For example, it is good for an electrical engineer to know physics and chemistry. But I still come back to the question of what the engineer is expected to do on the job. Being clear with these expectations reduces the focus to a subset of technical/job skills or performance skills.

Question 11: I'm not sure that I understand why you emphasize the difference between *job content* and *job context.* Can you explain further?

Sure. First, recall that *job context* reflects the broad identity of the organization. *Job content* contains the performance requirements for a specific job in the organization. It is desirable to have your HR processes reflect both the job content and job context to select people who can do specific jobs in your specific organization. This distinction is important because it enables you to have a way to reflect organizational identity and strategy, along with specific job requirements, in your HR systems.

Here is a practical example. Your CEO wants to be sure that all of your associates are screened to see whether they will fit into your organizational culture. Let's say that she wants everyone to be interviewed on *commitment to excellence.* So you create a structured interview that is administered to all candidates, regardless of the job. This sounds pretty logical and simple to do.

The problem emerges when you interview candidates to fit the culture but don't ask questions that reveal whether they can do their specific jobs. Even if everyone you hired has a commitment to excellence, there still may be people who can't do their jobs because they can't analyze data, organize their work, cope with conflict, assert themselves, and so forth. There was an error in selecting people only based on fit. The interview should also have contained questions relating to tasks that the candidate was to do on the job.

Summary and Conclusion

The best answers to questions about core competencies, capabilities, core values, and priorities come from real experiences in applying them. Today, each answer is just an opinion at one point in time. However, the big question for the future will be: *How can I link HR systems to my organization's identity?*

At present the most useful answers are those that emphasize

- A behavioral approach

- Job relatedness

- Nimbleness

- Open mindedness

Ironically, I just mentioned some attributes! Oh well, this may be another opportunity to operationalize a competency.

Resource A:
A Structured Interview

Position _____ Consultant/Trainer

Date _____

Name of candidate _____

Name of interviewer _____

The Performance Skills to be evaluated include:

	Very strong evidence skill not present	Strong evidence skill not present	Some evidence skill is present	Strong evidence skill is present	Very strong evidence skill is present	Insufficient evidence for or against skill
1. Spoken communication	☐	☐	☐	☐	☐	☐
2. Assertiveness	☐	☐	☐	☐	☐	☐
3. Analytical problem solving	☐	☐	☐	☐	☐	☐
4. Written communication	☐	☐	☐	☐	☐	☐
5. Organization and planning	☐	☐	☐	☐	☐	☐
6. Decision making and problem solving	☐	☐	☐	☐	☐	☐

Anchors

← Anchors →

The Technical/Job Skills to be evaluated include:

	Very strong evidence skill not present	Strong evidence skill not present	Some evidence skill is present	Strong evidence skill is present	Very strong evidence skill is present	Insufficient evidence for or against skill
1. Knowledge of human resource practices	☐	☐	☐	☐	☐	☐
2. Technology usage	☐	☐	☐	☐	☐	☐
3. Presentation	☐	☐	☐	☐	☐	☐
4. Sales skills	☐	☐	☐	☐	☐	☐
5. Product knowledge	☐	☐	☐	☐	☐	☐

Recommendation: Hire/promote _____ Not hire/promote _____

Reason for recommendation: _____

_____

_____

Spoken communications: Able to clearly present information through the spoken word; influences or persuades others through oral presentation in positive or negative circumstances; listens well.

Very strong evidence skill is not present	Strong evidence skill is not present	Some evidence skill is present	Strong evidence skill is present	Very strong evidence skill is present
---- x ----------- x ---------- x ---------- x ---------- x -----				

Less able to influence others	Adequate ability to influence others	Skilled at influencing others
Muffled, hesitant, or stammering speech	No speech problems	Clear articulate speech
Talks about self rather than others	Talks about self and others	Talks about others interests
Has stage fright, freezes up	Passable as a speaker	Skill in public speaking
Poor listener	Adequate listener	Listens well

Probes

What has been your experience in giving explanations or instructions to another person? Feel free to talk about your experiences in management, training, or coaching others.

What have been your experiences in making presentations or speeches to small or large groups? What has been your most successful experience in speech making?

Tell me about a time when your active listening skills really paid off for you— maybe a time when other people missed the key idea in what was being expressed.

Tell me about a time when your language and speaking skills really worked for you on the job. Feel free to use either a supervisory or nonsupervisory example.

Interpretive Guides

Did the candidate make a clear, confident presentation in a manner consistent with the listener's needs and abilities? Was there little preparation or fear and anxiety about the presentation?

Did the candidate make a well-planned, tasteful presentation, perhaps involving use of visuals, appropriate examples, or written speeches? Was there a lack of presentation experience, fear of public speaking, poor self-expression, or little awareness of presentation techniques?

Did the candidate use restatement, paraphrasing, or a reflection of thoughts or feelings to improve understanding? Was there a failure to pay attention, anger, or a judgmental approach that interfered with understanding the message?

Did the candidate express an idea clearly, perhaps involving careful choice of words, gestures, or stories? Was there an absence of preplanning or little choice of words, impulsiveness, or withdrawal?

Assertiveness: Able to maturely express one's feelings and opinions in spite of disagreement; accurately communicates to others regardless of their status or position.

Very strong evidence skill is not present	Strong evidence skill is not present	Some evidence skill is present	Strong evidence skill is present	Very strong evidence skill is present
---- x -----------	x ----------	x ----------	x ----------	x -----

Tends to withdraw	Average level of interaction	Feels free to express opinions
Overreacts to conflict	Some skill with conflict management	Manages conflict well
Fears disagreement	Occasionally intimidated	Rarely intimidated
Socially immature	Adequate social maturity	Socially mature
Fears disagreement	Copes with disagreement constructively	Manages disagreement

Probes

It is pretty realistic to say that no job is completely free of conflict. Tell me about a time when you were able to express your opinions maturely in spite of disagreements or objections.

Give me an example of a time when you had to be assertive in giving directions to others.

Describe a time when you commun-icated something unpleasant or diffi-cult to say to your manager or work team. How did you assert yourself?

Describe a time when you had to sell an idea to your boss, authority figure, or technical expert.

Interpretive Guides

Did the candidate directly state an opinion without having been abusive, harsh, apologetic, or defensive? Was there an emotional expression of an opinion or failure to express an opinion to avoid conflict?

Did the candidate give firm, clear direction, perhaps with concern for another's feelings? Was there an emotional reaction such as anger or anxiety?

Did the candidate accurately and tactfully express a fact or opinion on a sensitive or important issue? Was there avoidance of an issue, passive aggression, or an aggressive or tactless presentation?

Did the candidate make an honest, well-planned presentation including benefit statements? Were there responses to objections and guidance to a decision? Was there a dislike for selling an idea, dishonesty or distor-tion, withdrawal or passivity, or bragging or pressure?

Analytical problem solving: Able to use a systematic approach in solving problems through analysis of problem and evaluation of alternate solutions; uses logic, mathematics, or other problem-solving tools in data analysis or in generating solutions.

Very strong evidence skill is not present	Strong evidence skill is not present	Some evidence skill is present	Strong evidence skill is present	Very strong evidence skill is present
---- x -----------	-- x ----------	-- x ----------	-- x ----------	-- x -----

Not analytical	Sometimes analytical	Uses analytical skills
Less systematic in problem solving	May use systematic approach	Systematically attacks problems
Builds a single-solution strategy	May explore multiple solutions	Defines alternate courses of action
Fails to trouble-shoot solutions	Usually trouble-shoots solutions	Regularly trouble-shoots solutions
Prone to making assumptions	Usually questions assumptions	Regularly questions assumptions

Probes

Tell me about a time when you were systematic in identifying potential problems at work. Feel free to showcase your analytical skills.

Describe a time when you were proud of your ability to use your mathematical knowledge or research techniques to solve a problem.

Give me an example of any time when you used tools such as survey data, library research, or statistics as important contributors to the definition of a specific problem.

To what extent has your past work required you to be skilled in the analysis of technical reports or information? Pick any specific experience that would highlight your skills in this area and describe it in detail.

Interpretive Guides

Did the candidate anticipate and identify a problem, then collect data and analyze it? Was there a lack of anticipation or preparation, or use of a trial-and-error approach?

Did the candidate conduct or direct work that used research designs or statistics or mathematics? Was there use of only basic clerical skills or elementary mathematics as directed by someone else?

Did the candidate have a primary role in research design, formal data collection, and interpretation? Was there acceptance of questionable information or assumptions, or over-dependence on others?

Did the candidate conduct a close review of detailed technical information, requiring a professional education or training to understand? Was there a superficial or incomplete review of information, perhaps covering materials such as popular magazines?

Written communication: Able to write clearly and effectively present ideas and to document activities; able to read and interpret written information.

Very strong evidence skill is not present	Strong evidence skill is not present	Some evidence skill is present	Strong evidence skill is present	Very strong evidence skill is present
---- X ------------ X ---------- X ---------- X ---------- X -----				
Little or no work-related writing experience		Some work-related writing experience		Much work-related writing experience
Rarely uses written word to communicate		Recognizes value of written communication		Often uses written word to communicate
Limited skill with writing equipment		Some skill with writing equipment		Skilled with writing equipment
Sees little value in documentation		Recognizes value of documentation		Generates or uses documentation

Probes

In some jobs it is necessary to document work thoroughly, in writing. For example, documentation might be necessary to prove you did your job correctly or to train another person to do it. Give me an example of your experience in this area.

Tell me about the most complex information you have had to read—perhaps involving research you had to complete. To what extent did this project test your comprehension skills and technical knowledge? Be specific.

This job will require you to spend a large amount of time writing. Tell me about your writing experiences that you think will contribute to your ability to do this job well

Describe your experiences in editing manuscripts, articles, documents, or any other form of written communication. Be specific.

Interpretive Guides

Did the candidate emphasize accuracy in writing a description of an important activity? Was there organization of one's papers or documents, or presentation of required documents, without writing?

Did the candidate read and perhaps reread complex information (that would typically be covered by a college graduate working in a technical field) to ensure comprehension? Was there skill in reading and comprehending very basic instructions?

Did the candidate demonstrate writing skill and time commitment, perhaps as evidenced by publication? Was there little skill or interest in writing?

Did the candidate use understanding or comprehension, along with grammatical rules, perhaps leading to suggestions for creatively rewriting text? Was there little confidence or skill in use of proper grammar, punctuation, or spelling, and excuses for avoidance of writing?

Organization and planning: Able to organize or schedule people or tasks; able to develop realistic action plans while being sensitive to time constraints and resource availability.

Very strong evidence skill is not present	Strong evidence skill is not present	Some evidence skill is present	Strong evidence skill is present	Very strong evidence skill is present
---- x -----------	x ----------	x ----------	x ----------	x -----

Rarely uses written plans	Occasionally uses written plans	Uses written plans to guide activities
Little time management skill	Some skill in time management	Skilled in a time-management system
Disorganized	Generally organized	Highly organized
Resists the use of plans	Responds to plans made by others	Structures action plans
Little evidence of planning	Makes to-do lists and near-term plans	Makes long- and short-range plans

Probes

Give me an example of a time in which you were effective in doing away with the "constant emergencies" and "surprises" in your work climate. How did your planning help you deal with the unexpected?

Time management has become a necessary factor in personal productivity. Give me an example of any time management skill you have learned and applied at work. What resulted from use of the skill?

Give me an example from your working history that demonstrates your ability to organize and maintain a system of records to facilitate your work.

Getting results at work often entails spelling out detailed action plans. Tell me about how you used realistic schedules and timetables to generate a plan leading to a specific goal.

Interpretive Guides

Did the candidate use fact-finding, planning, organization, or training to prevent, or prepare for, emergencies? Was there a lack of preparation to do a job or project, or perhaps a tendency to deal with surprises or emergencies as they occurred?

Did the candidate have a strategy for using time management techniques across a variety of situations? Was work time used primarily for socializing or pleasant activity, with little emphasis on productivity?

Did the candidate initiate or show commitment to a systematic method for organization or record keeping? Was there ineffective record keeping, overconfidence in memory, or dependence on others?

Did the candidate formally define realistic and measurable objectives? Was there a trivial, near-term, or general objective, skepticism about the value of having objectives, or dependence on others to set objectives?

Decision making and problem solving: Able to take action in solving problems while exhibiting judgment and a realistic understanding of issues; able to use reason, even when dealing with emotional topics.

Very strong evidence skill is not present	Strong evidence skill is not present	Some evidence skill is present	Strong evidence skill is present	Very strong evidence skill is present
----x-----------	---x----------	--- x ----------	--- x ----------	--- x -----

Lets personal bias influence decisions	Generally objective	Regularly shows objective attitude
Rarely asks "why?"	Sometimes asks "why?"	Isolates problem causes
Poor judgment	Reasonably good judgment	Sound judgment
Bases decisions on emotions	Generally reasonable	Regularly bases decisions on facts
Generates impractical solutions	Usually generates practical solutions	Makes decisions that solve problems

Probes

When we get emotionally involved in a problem situation, it is often very difficult to be objective. Tell me about a time when you were proud of your ability to be objective even though you were emotional about a problem situation.

In many problem situations, it is often tempting to jump to a conclusion to build a solution quickly. Tell me about a time when you resisted this temptation and thoroughly obtained all facts associated with the problem before coming to a decision.

Tell me about a time when your understanding of issues associated with a problem provided you with a foundation for generating a good solution.

Even though you may be dealing with a complex problem, it is often important to use a commonsense approach in making a decision; not all analytical solutions will seem practical. Tell me about a time when your common sense paid off for you.

Interpretive Guides

Did the candidate observe behavior, collect facts, or use analytical results to draw a conclusion? Were there feelings that interfered with observation, collection of facts, or interpretation of them?

Did the candidate gain accurate information and analyze it to make a good decision, perhaps despite pressure to make a decision quickly? Was there an absence of fact finding, a reflex action, or impulsiveness in making a decision?

Did the candidate use a systematic approach, perhaps involving a written problem statement, casual analysis, solution criteria, review of each option's problems, or action taken? Were there emotional assumptions, poor judgment, or trial-and-error without forethought?

Did the candidate make an effective decision, particularly in light of practical opportunities or constraints? Was there a lack of effectiveness or great inefficiency, perhaps accompanied by insecurity, resistance, rigidity, withdrawal, or dependency?

Technical Skill Questions

Knowledge of Human Resource Practices

Able to apply knowledge of typical customer practices and needs, EEO law, including the ADA, and assessment tools.

1. Describe a time when your understanding of laws related to human resource processes was instrumental in helping you provide an effective solution.

2. Describe your experience with coordinating recruiting/selection.

Technology Usage

Able to use various computer software, e-mail, and other related technology applications for the office.

1. Summarize your experience with a customer contact management software program.

2. Summarize your experience with wordprocessing and spreadsheets.

3. Describe a time when you used technology to expedite a project.

Presentation

Able to deliver seminars, speeches, or presentations.

1. Describe a time when you used a seminar or training workshop as a springboard toward additional sales or to further a program or process in the workplace. How did you make the seminar work for you?

2. Describe the types of programs/presentations you have delivered, focusing on the areas of interviewing, performance management, and employee development.

Sales Skills

Able to execute specific sales techniques.

1. Describe a time when you used a sales model or innovative sales technique to advance a sale or promote an idea or program.

2. Describe any position you've had in which you had to sell a product or service, reach new goals, and/or do forecasting.

3. Describe a time when you were able to sell a complex concept or project to somebody.

Product Knowledge

Able to display knowledge of course material and explain it or adapt it to customer needs.

1. Describe a time when your thorough understanding of a service, program, or process you were implementing or selling helped you meet a customer's needs.

2. Describe the most challenging time you had to modify course materials or delivery to meet a specific customer goal.

Resource B:
A Highly Structured Interview

Position <u>Consultant/Trainer</u> Name of candidate _____

Date _____ Name of interviewer _____

The Performance Skills		*Ratings*
Spoken communication	Question 1	_____
	Question 2	_____
Assertiveness	Question 3	_____
	Question 4	_____
Analytical problem solving	Question 5	_____
	Question 6	_____
Written communication	Question 7	_____
	Question 8	_____
Organization and planning	Question 9	_____
	Question 10	_____
Decision making and problem solving	Question 11	_____
	Question 12	_____
	Total:	_____

The technical/job skills to be evaluated include*

1. Knowledge of human resource practices   4. Sales skills
2. Technology usage   5. Product knowledge
3. Presentation

Recommendation: Hire/promote _____ Not hire/promote _____

Reason for recommendation: _____

*Highly structured technical skills questions are not provided with this interview. They would, however, assume the same format as the highly structured performance skills questions.

Question 1: What has been your experience in giving spoken explanations or instructions to another person? Feel free to talk about your experiences in management, training, or coaching others.

Skill—Spoken communication: Able to clearly present information through the spoken word; influences or persuade others through oral presentation in positive or negative circumstances; listens well.

Guidelines and Word Themes: The Candidate's Response Shows . . .

5. Use of clear, confident presentation in a manner consistent with listeners' needs/abilities. Attention may have been given systematically to factors such as preparation, effective mix of logic and emotion, respect for the listener, and communicating with a difficult person or large group.

3. Commonsense preparation, usually carried out by most people in similar circumstances, particularly with individuals and/or small groups. There may have been discomfort or aloofness in dealing with hostile/difficult situations.

1. An absence of preparation and/or presence of fear/anxiety in presentation. There may have been such things as poor taste, stammering, overtalking, freezing up, and/or focus on oneself as opposed to the listener.

Notes:

Question 2: What have been your experiences in making presentations or speeches to small or large groups? What has been your most successful experience in speech making?

Skill—Spoken communication: Able to clearly present information through the spoken word; able to influence or persuade others through oral presentation in positive or negative circumstances; listens well.

Guidelines and Word Themes: The Candidate's Response Shows . . .

5. A well-planned, tasteful presentation, perhaps involving use of visuals, appropriate examples and/or written speeches. There may have been realistic tension that motivated preparation, but little anxiety during the presentation.

3. Commonsense preparation to speak to small groups but not large audiences. The preparation may not have eliminated presentation anxiety.

1. A lack of presentation experience, fear/anxiety of public speaking, poor self-expression, and/or little awareness of presentation techniques. There may be a stated resistance/refusal to make presentations and/or speeches.

Notes:

Question 3: It is pretty realistic to say that no job is completely free of conflict. Tell me about a time when you were able to express your opinions maturely in spite of disagreements or objections.

Skill—Assertiveness: Able to maturely express one's feelings and opinions in spite of disagreement; accurately communicates to others regardless of their status or position.

Guidelines and Word Themes: The Candidate's Response Shows . . .

5. An honest, direct statement of an opinion/feeling without having been abusive/harsh/apologetic/defensive. High self-confidence may have been coupled with verbal persistence.

3. Negative feelings, perhaps resulting in a lack of firmness, indirect expression of an opinion and/or hesitation. The negative feelings may have led to an accusatory/irritable expression of an opinion.

1. Either an emotional, harsh way of expressing an opinion or avoidance of expressing an opinion in order to avoid conflict. There may have been either a fight-or-flight response.

Notes:

Question 4: Give me an example of a time when you had to be assertive in giving directions to others.

Skill—Assertiveness: Able to maturely express one's feelings and opinions in spite of disagreement; accurately communicates to others regardless of their status or position.

Guidelines and Word Themes: The Candidate's Response Shows . . .

5. Comfort in giving firm, clear direction, perhaps along with concern for another's feelings. There may have been a combination of directness and tact.

3. Discomfort in giving instructions, possibly because of a desire to be liked and/or a fear of rejection/conflict. There may have been a hesitation to be explicit or may have given unclear direction to reduce the possibility of rejection/conflict.

1. An emotional reaction such as anger/anxiety/depression, perhaps with insecurity with a directive role. Conflict was handled either aggressively or submissively, reflecting either an autocratic or dependent style.

Notes:

Question 5: Tell me about a time when you were systematic in identifying potential problems at work. Feel free to showcase your analytical skills.

Skill—Analytical Problem Solving: Able to use a systematic approach in solving problems through analysis of problem and evaluation of alternate solutions; uses logic, mathematics, or other problem-solving tools in data analysis or in generating solutions.

Guidelines and Word Themes: The Candidate's Response Shows . . .

5. Anticipation and problem identification, followed by a series of data collection and deductive steps. There was more than practical judgment, as steps were taken for gathering information and using logic to define the causes or components of a problem.

3. Involvement in systematic fact-finding, perhaps as a member of a team or as an individual contributor. There may have been use of practical reasoning, perhaps with a focus on an immediate, perhaps standard, course of action.

1. Lack of anticipation/preparation and/or the use of a trial-and-error approach for problem solving. The solution may have been obvious at best, random at worst, perhaps involving over-dependence on other(s).

Notes:

Question 6: Describe a time when you were proud of your ability to use your mathematical knowledge or research techniques to solve a problem.

Skill—Analytical Problem Solving: Able to use a systematic approach in solving problems through analysis of problem and evaluation of alternate solutions; uses logic, mathematics, or other problem-solving tools in data analysis or in generating solutions.

Guidelines and Word Themes: The Candidate's Response Shows . . .

5. Use of sophisticated research design and/or statistical/mathematical procedures. Work was independently conducted by the candidate, perhaps with some input from collegial/team relationships. There may have been thorough documentation of previous research in the area.

3. Use of standard mathematical procedures, perhaps involving basic business math and/or a dependence on others for design and analysis. There may have been an identification/summary of others' research.

1. Use of basic clerical skills/elementary math as directed by another. The candidate may have had a role in a project that did not allow for any real decision making.

Notes:

Question 7: In some jobs it is necessary to document work thoroughly, in writing. For example, documentation might be necessary to prove you did your job correctly or to train another person to do it. Give me an example of your experiences in this area.

Skill—Written Communication: Able to write clearly and present ideas effectively and to document activities; able to read and interpret written information.

Guidelines and Word Themes: The Candidate's Response Shows . . .

5. Accuracy in writing a description of an important activity. The documentation may have taken place at the same time as the activity.

3. Compliance with documentation needs/expectations by writing. The activity may have been a fairly routine report or summary, using basic business writing skills.

1. Organization of one's paper or documents and/or presentation of required documentation, without writing. There may have been some resistance to documentation and/or an excuse to why it was not carried out.

Notes:

Question 8: Tell me about the most complex information you have had to read—perhaps involving research you had to complete. To what extent did this project test your comprehension skills and technical knowledge? Be specific.

Skill—Written Communication: Able to write clearly and present ideas effectively and to document activities; able to read and interpret written information.

Guidelines and Word Themes: The Candidate's Response Shows . . .

5. Reading and rereading complex information to ensure comprehension. The content of what was read would typically be covered by a college graduate working in a technical field.

3. Reading skill comparable with that of most reasonably educated persons in the United States. Most high school graduates could have read the information and comprehended its meaning.

1. Skill in reading and comprehending very basic instructions. Persons at this level would have felt comfortable reading a newspaper.

Notes:

Question 9: Give me an example of a time in which you felt you were effective in doing away with the constant emergencies and surprises in your work climate. How did your planning help you deal with the unexpected?

Skill—Organization and Planning: Able to organize or schedule people or tasks; develops realistic action plans while being sensitive to time constraints and resource availability.

Guidelines and Word Themes: The Candidate's Response Shows . . .

5. Use of planning/organization/training to prevent or prepare for emergencies. A rationale for the plan may have been developed, based on an understanding of the causes of emergencies in that area of work.

3. Preparation to do a job/project without identification of potential causes of problems. There may have been standard planning/job setup without anticipation of surprises/emergencies.

1. Lack of preparation to do a job/project. Surprises/emergencies may have simply been dealt with as they emerged, with little effort being given to prevention.

Notes:

Question 10: Time management has become a necessary factor in personal productivity. Give me an example of any time management skill you have learned and applied at work. What resulted from use of the skill?

Skill—Organization and Planning: Able to organize or schedule people or tasks; develops realistic action plans while being sensitive to time constraints and resource availability.

Guidelines and Word Themes: The Candidate's Response Shows . . .

5. A strategy for using a combination of time management techniques. There may have been tasks such as goal setting, organization of work, setting priorities, meeting management, and avoidance of distractions.

3. Use of one or two time management techniques to solve a single problem. There may have been casual awareness of the value of time and/or how to capitalize on even small periods of time.

1. Use of work time primarily for socializing/pleasant activity, with little emphasis on the productive value of time. Participation may have been an excuse for a lack of self-discipline or time management. Or there may have been dependence on another person/work procedures to manage time.

Notes:

Question 11: When we get emotionally involved in a problem situation, it is often very difficult to be objective. Tell me about a time when you were proud of your ability to be objective even though you were emotional about a problem situation.

Skill—Decision Making and Problem Solving: Able to take action in solving problems while exhibiting judgment and a realistic understanding of issues; able to use reason, even when dealing with emotional topics.

Guidelines and Word Themes: The Candidate's Response Shows . . .

5. Observation of behavior/collection of facts/use of analytical results to draw a conclusion. There may have been concern for measurement effectiveness, analysis of the causes of the problem, and emotional self-discipline. The action taken may have been different from the candidate's feelings.

3. An attempt to be objective despite emotional interference with objective thinking. The effort to control one's feelings may have diverted attention away from gathering information or using logic.

1. Feelings interfered with observations, collection of facts, and interpretation of them. There may have been a preference for using feelings over objective information or withdrawal/overdependence when a decision was needed.

Notes:

Question 12: In many problem situations, it is often tempting to jump to a conclusion to build a solution quickly. Tell me about a time when you resisted this temptation and thoroughly obtained all facts associated with the problem before coming to a decision.

Skill—Decision Making and Problem Solving: Able to take action in solving problems while exhibiting judgment and a realistic understanding of issues; able to use reason, even when dealing with emotional topics.

Guidelines and Word Themes: The Candidate's Response Shows . . .

5. Gaining accurate information and analysis of it to make a good decision. The gathering and review of information may have been carefully done despite pressure to make the decision quickly.

3. A relatively standard decision that could have been made by most adequately trained people in the job. But pressure may have interfered with gathering information, or the method of gathering information may have been more anecdotal than systematic.

1. An absence of fact-finding, a reflex action, or impulsivity in a decision. There may have been a strong emotional reaction that made the candidate ineffective, or there may have been an excuse for the action taken.

Notes:

Resource C:
A Task-Based Appraisal Form

Position <u>Consultant/Trainer</u>   Name of candidate _____

Date _____   Name of interviewer _____

Performance Skills
1. Spoken communication
2. Assertiveness
3. Analytical problem solving
4. Written communication
5. Organization and planning
6. Decision making and problem solving

Technical/job Skills
1. Knowledge of human resource practices
2. Technology usage
3. Presentation
4. Sales skills
5. Product knowledge

Overall Ratings

Goals for Coaching: _____

_____

_____

_____

_____

_____

Spoken Communication: Clearly present information through the spoken word; influence or persuade others through oral presentation in positive or negative circumstances; listen well.

☐ Give spoken explanations or instructions to associates regarding appropriate means so as to delegate work.

☐ Make presentations or speeches to help clarify understanding, or to further organizational goals.

☐ Demonstrate listening skill by restating what was heard to confirm others' understanding of needs/requirements.

☐ Display effective language and speaking skills to professionally and successfully communicate needs or requirements to others.

Assertiveness: Maturely express one's opinions and feelings in spite of disagreement; accurately communicate to others regardless of their status or position.

☐ Maturely express opinions or concerns, in spite of disagreement, to effectively communicate important information or opinions in meetings.

☐ Assertively give terse, explicit directions to others to ensure correct understanding and compliance.

☐ Assertively disagree with superiors as necessary to stimulate thinking and communicate important feedback/information/opinions.

☐ Present new ideas to authority figures to inform, stimulate thinking, or promote creative strategies, even if there probably would be resistance.

Analytical Problem Solving: Use a systematic approach in solving problems through analysis of problem and evaluation of alternate solutions; use logic, mathematics, or other problem-solving tools in data analysis or in generating solutions.

☐ Systematically identify potential problems when designing systems/products, using brainstorming techniques, cost/benefits analyses, and so on, to reduce the chances of unnecessary problems. Use mathematics, statistics, or research techniques for testing alternative strategies to solve complex problems.

Define problems, using survey data/library research/statistics to uncover valuable areas of opportunity/improvement.

Analyze technical reports or information to make informed decisions.

Written Communication: Write clearly and present ideas effectively and document activities; read and interpret written information.

Thoroughly document work in writing to provide an audit trail of activity that can be meaningfully referred to later.

Read complex information, often interpreting research analyses and results, to assess success of specified processes or strategies.

Spend a large amount of time writing to produce high volumes of text/manual/brochure copy within customer-specified time frames.

Edit manuscripts, articles, or other documents to identify and correct errors before publication or use.

Organization and Planning: Organize or schedule people or tasks; develop realistic action plans while being sensitive to time constraints and resource availability.

Develop plans to deal with unexpected events to facilitate effective functioning during machine downtime, materials shortages, and so on.

Use time management skills, such as delegating or having stand-up meetings to minimize potential distractions.

Organize and maintain a system of records to enable easy access to customer histories.

Make realistic schedules and timetables, using management by objectives to target available resources toward specific organizationally defined goals.

Decision Making and Problem Solving: Take action in solving problems while exhibiting judgment and a realistic understanding of issues; use reason, even when dealing with emotional topics.

▢ Make sensitive management decisions, remaining objective even when dealing with emotional topics such as personnel issues, to accomplish departmental objectives.

▢ Get the facts necessary for making effective decisions, avoiding the temptation to jump to conclusions and despite pressure to act, to prevent valuable resources from being misspent.

▢ Discuss issues with, and get facts/opinions from, relevant individuals or groups to learn the real issues behind problems and subsequently provide optimal solutions.

▢ Make management decisions on an ongoing basis, using common sense as a guide, to maintain a continuous flow of operations.

Knowledge of Human Resource Practices: Able to apply knowledge of typical customer practices and needs, EEO law, including the ADA, and assessment tools.

▢ Apply human resource laws to problem solving to maintain fair and legally compliant operations.

▢ Coordinate recruitment and selection efforts to hire high performers as efficiently as possible.

Technology Usage: Able to use various computer software, e-mail, and other related technology applications for the office.

▢ Use customer contact management software programs to organize, plan, and keep track of interactions with customers.

▢ Use Microsoft Word, Excel, and other software programs to expedite composition and analysis.

▢ Use technology in the form of the internet, statistics, software, and so on to generate results with an unusually high degree of efficiency.

Presentation: Able to deliver seminars or other services.

☐ Use seminars as springboards toward additional sales to efficiently merge sales and delivery efforts.

☐ Deliver programs/presentations related to interviewing, performance management, and employee development to help organizations become more proficient in human resource programs.

Sales Skills: Able to execute specific sales techniques.

☐ Use the SPIN model and other techniques when selling to take advantage of researched and proven sales approaches.

☐ Forecast sales, set sales goals based on the forecasts, and attain sales goals to grow in an orderly, controlled, and manageable fashion.

☐ Sell complex concepts to others by simplifying them and presenting the benefits to find testing grounds for new services.

Product Knowledge: Able to display knowledge of course material; able to explain it or adapt it to customer needs.

☐ Learn the intricate workings of the organization's programs to adapt them to clients' needs fluently.

☐ Modify course materials to adapt the course to specific clients' situational needs.

References

Abrahams, J. *The Mission Statement Book: 301 Corporate Mission Statements from America's Top Companies*. San Francisco: Ten Speed Press, 1995.

American Compensation Association. *Raising the Bar*. Scottsdale, Ariz.: American Compensation Association, May 1996.

American Educational Research Association, American Psychological Association, and National Council on Measurement in Education. *Standards for Educational and Psychological Testing*. Washington, D.C.: American Psychological Association, 1985.

Bandura, A. *Social Foundations of Thought and Action: A Social Cognitive Theory*. Englewood Cliffs, N.J.: Prentice Hall, 1986.

Barrett, G. V., and Depinet, R. L. "A Reconsideration of Testing for Competence Rather Than for Intelligence." *American Psychologist*, 1991, *46* (10), 1012–1024.

Barrick, M. R., and Mount, M. K. "The Big Five Personality Dimensions and Job Performance: A Meta-Analysis." *Personnel Psychology*, Spring 1991, *44*, 1–26.

Benardin, J. H., and Beatty, R. W. *Performance Appraisal: Assessing Human Behavior at Work*. Boston: Kent, 1984.

Boyatzis, R. E. *The Competent Manager: A Model for Effective Performance*. New York: Wiley, 1982.

Boyatzis, R. E., Cowen, S. S., and Kolb, D. A. *Innovation in Professional Education: Steps on a Journey from Teaching to Learning*. San Francisco: Jossey-Bass, 1995.

Campion, M. A., Campion, J. E., and Hudson, P. "Structured Interviewing: A Note on Incremental Validity and Alternative Question Types." *Journal of Applied Psychology*, 1994, *79*(6), 998–1002.

Campion, M. A., Palmer, D. K., and Campion, J. E. "A Review of Structure in the Selection Interview." *Personnel Psychology*, 1997, *50*, 1–46.

Civil Rights Act, 1991. U.S. Code. Vol. 42, sec. 20002-e(k)(1)(A)(I).

Dalton, G., and Thompson, P. *Novations*. Provo, UT: Novation, 1993.

Equal Opportunity Commission. *Americans with Disabilities Act Employment Regulations*. Title 29, Code of Federal Regulations, Part 1630.2(n). Washington, DC: GPO, effective July 26, 1992.

Fleishman, E., and Reilly, M. E. *Handbook of Human Abilities: Definitions, Measurements, and Job Task Requirements*. Palo Alto, Calif.: Consulting Psychologists Press, 1992.

Gagné, R. M., and Medsker, K. L. *The Conditions of Learning: Training Applications*. New York: Harcourt Brace College Publishers, 1996.

Gilbert, T., and Gilbert, M., "The Science of Winning." *Training*, August 1988, 25(8), 33–40.

Goldman, S. L., Nagel, R. N., and Preiss, K. *Agile Competitors and Virtual Organizations*. New York: Van Nostrand Reinhold, 1995.

Gollub, W. L., Campion, J. E., Malos, S. B., Roehling, M. V., and Campion, M. A. "Employment Interview on Trial: Linking Interview Structure with Litigation Outcomes." *Journal of Applied Psychology*, 1997, 82(6), 900–912.

Green, P. C. *Get Hired! Winning Strategies to Ace the Interview*. Austin, Tex.: Bard Books, 1996.

Green, P. C., Alter, P., and Carr, A. F. "Development of Standard Anchors for Scoring Generic Past-Behavior Questions in Structured Interviews." *International Journal of Selection and Assessment*, Oct. 1993, 1, 203–212.

Grote, D. *The Complete Guide to Performance Appraisal*. New York: AMACOM, 1996.

Hamel, G. "The Concept of Core Competence." In G. Hamel and A. Heene (Eds.). *Competence-Based Competition*. New York: Wiley, 1994, 11–33.

Hamel, G., and Prahalad, C. K. *Competing for the Future*. Boston: Harvard Business School Press, 1994.

Harvey, R. O. "Job Analysis." In M. D. Dunnette and L. M. Hough (eds.), *The Handbook of Industrial and Organizational Psychology*, Vol. 2 (2nd ed.). Palo Alto, Calif.: Consulting Psychologists Press, 1991.

Hedge, J. W., and Borman, W. C. "Changing Conceptions and Practices in Performance Appraisal." In A. Howard (ed.), *The Changing Nature of Work*. San Francisco: Jossey-Bass, 1995.

Hellervik, L. W., Hazucha, J. F., and Schneider, R. J. "Behavior Change: Models, Methods, and a Review of Evidence." In M. D. Dunnette and L. M. Hough (eds.), *The Handbook of Industrial and Organizational Psychology*, Vol. 3. (2nd ed.) Palo Alto, Calif.: Consulting Psychologists Press, 1992.

Hunter, J. E., and Hunter, R. F. "Validity and Utility of Alternative Predictors of Job Performance." *Psychological Bulletin*, 1984, *96*, 72–98.

Industry Report 1997: A Statistical Picture of Employer Sponsored Training in the United States. *Training*, 1997, *34*(10), 49–56.

Janz, T. "Initial Comparisons of Patterned Behavior Description Interviews versus Unstructured Interviews." *Journal of Applied Psychology*, 1982, *67*, 577–580.

Kirkpatrick, D. L. *Evaluating Training Programs: The Four Levels*. San Francisco: Berrett-Koehler, 1994.

Labovitz, G., and Rosansky, V. *The Power of Alignment: How Great Companies Stay Centered and Accomplish Extraordinary Things*. New York: Wiley, 1997.

Latham, G. "Behavioral Approaches to the Training and Learning Process." In I. L. Goldstein and Associates (eds.), *Training and Development in Organizations*. San Francisco: Jossey-Bass, 1989.

Latham, G. P., and Wexley, K. N. *Increasing Productivity through Performance Appraisal*. (2nd ed.) New York: Addison-Wesley, 1994.

Lawler, E. E. *The Ultimate Advantage: Creating the High-Involvement Organization*. San Francisco: Jossey-Bass, 1992.

Lawler, E. E. *From the Ground Up: Six Principles for Building the New Logic Corporation*. San Francisco: Jossey-Bass, 1996.

Lawler, E. E., and Ledford, G. "New Approaches to Organizing Competencies: Capabilities and the Decline of the Bureaucratic Model." In C. Cooper and S. Jackson (eds.), *Creating Tomorrow's Organizations: A Handbook for Future Research in Organizational Behavior*. Chichester, England: Wiley, 1997.

Locke, E. A., and Latham, G. P. *A Theory of Goal Setting and Task Performance*. (rev. 2nd ed.) Englewood Cliffs, N.J.: Prentice Hall, 1990.

Mager, R. F. *Preparing Instructional Objectives*. Belmont, Calif.: Davis S. Lake, 1984.

McClelland, D. C. "Testing for Competence Rather Than for 'Intelligence.'" *American Psychologist*, 1973, *28*, 1–4.

McDaniel, M. A., Whetzel, D. L., Schmidt, F. L., and Maurer, S. "The Validity of Employment Interviews: A Comprehensive Review and Meta-analysis." *Journal of Applied Psychology*, 1994, *79*, 599–616.

Mohrman, A. M. "Deming versus Performance Appraisal: Is There a Resolution?" In G. N. McLean, S. R. Damme, and R. A. Swanson (eds.), *Performance Appraisal: Perspectives on a Quality Management Approach: Fifth in the Theory-to-Practice Monograph Series*. Alexandria, Va.: American Society for Training and Development, 1990.

Morrisey, G. L. *On Planning: A Guide to Strategic Thinking: Building Your Planning Foundation.* San Francisco: Jossey-Bass, 1996.

Motowidlo, S. J., Carter, G. W., Dunnette, M. D., Tippins, N., Werner, S., Burnett, J. R., and Vaughan, M. J. "Studies of the Structured Behavioral Interview." *Journal of Applied Psychology,* 1992, *77,* 571–587.

Nanus, B. *Visionary Leadership.* San Francisco: Jossey-Bass, 1992.

Norling, R. A., and Pashley, S. "Identifying and Strengthening Core Values." *Managed Care Quarterly,* 1995, *3*(1), 11–28.

Obrien, M. J. *Personal Mastery Journal.* Milford, Ohio: Obrien Learning Systems, 1997.

Orpen, C. "Patterned Behavior Description Interviews versus Unstructured Interviews: A Comparative Validity Study." *Journal of Applied Psychology,* 1985, *70,* 774–776.

Owens, W. A. "Background Data." In M. D. Dunnette (Ed.). *Handbook of Industrial and Organizational Psychology* (1st ed.). Chicago: Rand McNally, 1976.

Peterson, N. G., Mumford, M. D., Borman, W. C., Jeanneret, P. R., and Fleishman, E. A. "Development of Prototype Occupational Information Network (O*NET)." Utah Department of Employment Security, 1995. (Contract number 94-542)

Pfeffer, J. *Competitive Advantage Through People: Unleashing the Power of the Workforce.* Boston: Harvard Business School Press, 1994.

Prahalad, C. K., and Hamel, G. "The Core Competence of the Corporation." *Harvard Business Review,* 1990, *68,* 79–93.

Pulakos, E. D., and Schmitt, N. "Experience-Based and Situational Interview Questions: Studies of Validity." *Personnel Psychology,* 1995, *48,* 289–308.

Robinson, D. G., and Robinson, J. C. *Training for Impact: How to Link Training to Business Needs and Measure the Results.* San Francisco: Jossey-Bass, 1989.

Rothwell, W. J., and Kazanas, H. C. *Mastering the Instructional Design Process: A Systematic Approach.* San Francisco: Jossey-Bass, 1992.

Sanchez, J. I. "From Documentation to Innovation: Reshaping Job Analysis to Meet Emerging Business Needs." *Human Resource Management Review,* 1994, *4*(1), 51–74.

Schein, E. H. "Deep Culture." In J. C. Glidewell (ed.), *Corporate Cultures: Research Implications for Human Resource Development.* Washington, D.C.: American Society for Training and Development, 1986.

Scholtes, P. R. *The Team Handbook: How to Use Teams to Improve Quality.* Madison, Wis.: Joiner Associates, 1988.

Scholtes, P. R. "An Elaboration on Deming's Teachings on Performance Appraisal." In G. N. McLean, S. R. Damme, and P. Senge. *The Fifth Discipline*. New York: Doubleday, 1990.

Society for Industrial and Organizational Psychology. *Principles for the Validation and Use of Personnel Selection Procedures*. (3rd ed.) College Park, Md.: Society for Industrial and Organizational Psychology, 1987.

Spencer, L. M., and Spencer, S. M. *Competence at Work*. New York: Wiley, 1993.

Stalk, G., and Hout, T. M. *Competing Against Time: How Time-Based Competition Is Reshaping Global Markets*. New York: Free Press, 1990.

Stalk, G., Evans, P., and Shulman, L. "Competing on Capabilities: The New Rules of Corporate Strategy." *The Harvard Business Review*, Mar.-Apr. 1992, 57–69. (Reprint no. 92209)

Tett, R. P., Jackson, D. N., and Rothstein, M. "Personality Measures as Predictors of Job Performance: A Meta-Analytic Review." *Personnel Psychology*, 1991, *44*, 703–742.

"Uniform Guidelines on Employee Selection Procedures." *Federal Register*, no. 43 (1978): 38290–38315.

U.S. Department of Labor. "The Secretary's Commission on Achieving Necessary Skills: What Work Requires of Schools: A SCANS Report for America 2000." Washington, D.C.: U.S. Department of Labor, 1991a.

U.S. Department of Labor. *Dictionary of Occupational Titles*. (4th ed.) Washington, D.C.: U.S. Department of Labor, 1991b.

U.S. Department of Labor. *The New D.O.T.: A Database of Occupational Titles for the Twenty-First Century*. Washington, D.C.: U.S. Department of Labor, 1993.

Walton, M. *Deming Management at Work*. New York: Perigee Books, 1991.

Weisner, W., and Cronshaw, S. "A Meta-Analytic Investigation of the Impact of Interview Format and Degree of Structure on the Validity of the Employment Interview." *Journal of Occupational Psychology*, 1988, *61*, 275–290.

Werner, J. M., and Bolino, M. C. "Explaining U.S. Courts of Appeals Decisions Involving Performance Appraisal: Accuracy, Fairness, and Validation." *Personnel Psychology*, 1997, *50*, 1–24.

Wetherbe, J. C. *The World on Time®: The 11 Management Principles That Made FedEx an Overnight Sensation*. Santa Monica, Calif.: Knowledge Exchange, 1996.

Whiteley, R., and Hessan, D. *Customer-Centered Growth: Five Proven Strategies for Building Competitive Advantage*. New York: Addison-Wesley, 1996.

Winters, D., and Latham, G. "The Effect of Learning versus Outcome Goals on a Simple versus a Complex Task." *Group and Organization Management*, June 1996, *21*(2), 236–250.

Zemkie, R. "The Corporate Coach." *Training*. Dec. 1996.

About Behavioral Technology, Inc.

Behavioral Technology is a training and consulting firm with offices in Memphis, Tennessee. Its premier product is its Behavioral Interviewing® System, which has been implemented in small and large organizations across the United States, Canada, and parts of Europe and Asia. Its growth products include recruiting, appraisal, coaching, and the development of linked competency systems.

In May 1998, Behavioral Technology merged with six other companies to form the first publicly traded performance skills training company, PROVANT. It is now traded on the NASDAQ exchange, giving it access to capital and technology that will be the foundation of future service to its clients. With over one thousand full-time employees and offices in Boston, New York, Washington, D.C., Atlanta, Dallas, Chicago, Hollywood, San Francisco, and Lansing, Michigan, PROVANT is positioned to be the international leader in training and development.

At the time of publication, the sister companies of PROVANT include

American Media—video training

Behavioral Technology—selection interviewing

Decker Communications—presentation skills

Executive Perspectives—strategic consulting and training

Gulliver Ritchie and Associates—Internet training

J. Howard and Associates—diversity

KC Resources—instructional design

Learning Science Systems—multimedia and instructional design

MOHR Retail—retail training

Novations—careers and competencies

Star Mountain—government training

Strategic Interactive—Intranet training

For inquiries about PROVANT companies, phone Behavioral Technology at 1 (800) 227-6855 or write to us at Behavioral Technology, Inc., 6260 Poplar, Memphis, TN 38119.

Index